SALT-FREE COOKING

Tempting tastes need not be sacrificed for the sake of good health.
Here is a collection of delicious dishes which are full of flavour —
without the use of a single grain of salt!

SALT-FREE COOKING

Recipes for Eating Well on a Low-Sodium Diet

by

JACKIE APPLEBEE

Illustrated by Kim Blundell

THORSONS PUBLISHERS LIMITED
Wellingborough, Northamptonshire

First published 1984

British Library Cataloguing in Publication Data

Applebee, Jackie
  Salt-free cookery.
  1. Salt-free diet
  I. Title
  641.5'632   RM237.8

ISBN 0-7225-0846-8

Printed and bound in Great Britain

CONTENTS

PREFACE

In teaching wholefood cookery I always encourage students to consider their salt intake by looking at the minimal need that the body has for it. The amount needed for fluid balance in the body is so small that to consume it in excess is very easy.

Acquiring a taste for salt is something you don't often notice, so in this book I have used no salt whatsoever and looked at herbs and spices as flavouring agents; even the baking powder is sodium free!

As a wholefood cookery teacher I have automatically used the basic principles of wholefoods, low-fat, sugar-free, fresh food, wholegrains and, above all, just food, the whole food and nothing but the food.

JACKIE APPLEBEE

INTRODUCTION

Salt, or table salt, as it is sometimes called, is sodium chloride. In writing about salt it is much clearer to refer to it as sodium chloride.

There are many references to salt through history, Homer called it 'divine', the Egyptians and Chinese worshipped it as a giver of life. Fishermen of the Suma district of Japan burnt seaweed to obtain salt. They did this by spreading the seaweeds on the beach, sprinkling them with seawater several times, drying them to condense the brine and burning the remainder to ashes. The ashes were placed in pots and mixed with fresh water, the salt then dissolved into the water which was dried until crystallized salt was produced. This ceremony has been replaced by modern methods, but the act of burning seaweed for salt still persists at the religious festivals of the Shiogama shrine in Miyagi. Roman soldiers were paid 'salt money': the Latin word for salt is *sal,* so this was the origin of the word 'salaries'. Greek workers were fed on salt fish, but it was the Romans who became highly skilled at mining and evaporating it from the sea. Sanskrit and its daughter languages have no common root word for salt.

Rudolf Ballentine M.D., in his book *Diet and Nutrition, a Holistic Approach* says that the oldest salt mines known to man were in the late Bronze Age, about 1,000 BC, in the Austrian Tyrol.

Salt today has no relevance to divinity, salary or even table placing at a meal, as was the case in the Middle Ages, where if you sat anywhere but at the high table you were classed as 'below the salt'. Whereas this expression was humiliating, today you could be very boastful if your diet was 'below the salt' level! This is because, over the years there has been more and more medical information presented about the danger of excess sodium in the diet.

What is Sodium?

Sodium is an alkali. It moves readily through water, which is obvious when you think about it because the large bulk of water surrounding the earth is of a saline solution. It is essentially a sodium solution containing huge quantities of chloride, and the combination of sodium and chloride is known as salt. The saline solution has been known for many years to support various plant and animal forms.

The adult body contains 75-100 grams of sodium chloride. Over half of it is in the blood plasma and fluids surrounding the cells. Only 10 per cent is held inside the cell and the remaining proportion forms part of the structure of the bone. Its most vital role is based on the fact that it is responsible for maintaining body water content.

Excess sodium drives out potassium. Potassium is the electrolyte inside the body's cells and sodium is the electrolyte outside the cell. If an excess of sodium chloride enters the liquid surrounding the cells it will absorb more fluid, simply by virtue of its concentration. The fluid will come from inside the cell, creating the feeling of puffiness and bloatedness. Evolution shows how the lower more primitive animals that existed in salty water did so because the inside of their cells had a higher concentration of sodium. Red blood cells however have a high potassium level and low sodium content in the ratio of 5:1. Any form of depletion of either sodium or potassium in the body affects the cells' ability to respond to various stimuli.

The body content is kept constant in that the salt gained from food is balanced by equal losses in the urine. Balance can be upset by excessive loss in perspiration (sweat) and although the kidneys reduce the quantity lost in urine to almost nil, the amount of sodium lost in sweat can exceed the day's intake.

In hot countries it is traditional to take salt tablets, but H. Mitchell, in his book *Nutrition and Climatic Stress II* writes that, after an initial period while the body adapts, very little sodium is lost through perspiration, but larger quantities of potassium *can* be lost from the body. People on low sodium diets give out very little sodium in their sweat and others, that have only the necessary daily intake, will have sweat of pure water.

Diarrhoea can also cause an imbalance as the sodium is not absorbed by the body. It is the hormones in the kidneys (in particular

Aldosterone) that conserve and regulate the removal of excessive sodium via the urine. The renal tubes in the kidneys can either re-absorb it, or pass it out. Excess salting of food can alter the tolerance level of sodium in the kidneys, thus straining it, just as no sodium at all can lead to kidney failure.

Some medical authorities feel that the individuals 'salt appetite' is determined by diet in the early months and years of weaning, and this has no relationship to sodium needs. Hence, one of the yeast extract firms can say, 'Once a *M*—baby, always a *M*—baby' as it seems a baby, or adult, can acquire a 'salt tooth' that is out of balance to requirements.

The Effects of Too Much Salt

Polynesians who boil their food in sea water to cook it show some incidence of raised blood-pressure, compared to those who cook their food in fresh water and do not add salt to their cooking. The 'salt-free cooking' group are free from high blood-pressure. The country with the highest incidence of strokes in the world is Japan, where the diet is high in sodium (salted fish, salty preserved foods like miso, soy sauce and umeboshi plums). One of the contributory factors to heart disease is high blood-pressure, which does not occur as a one-off thing when you oversalt the potatoes, it is a condition that builds up slowly. In the populations where high blood-pressure is unknown and blood-pressure decreases with age, Western ways have not been adopted and daily sodium intake is less than 500mg per day.

The salt content of baby food had to be reduced as it was proved that infant kidney failure resulted from high sodium levels.

Sodium and Potassium Content of Milk (per 100g)

	Sodium (Na)	Potassium
Human milk	14 mg	14 mg
Cow's milk	50 mg	95 mg
Goat's milk	40 mg	110 mg

Restricting sodium intake in babies and young children is a far greater preventative and easier to do than reducing salt intake once blood-pressure has started rising.

How Do We Eat Too Much Sodium?

Sodium intake is increased by adding salt to cooking, the consumption of cured meat, fish and especially processed meats like sausages, canned foods, cheese, bottled sauces, pickles, salad dressings, baking powder, monosodium glutamate, butter, margarine, peanut butter and carbonated waters. The sodium intake into the body is also much more out of balance when the potassium intake is low, and our daily consumption of potassium-rich foods has actually dropped considerably in recent years. Without potassium, glucose cannot be exchanged into energy.

The foods highest in potassium are: apples; broccoli; grapefruit; bananas; orange juice; spinach; lettuce; cantaloupe melon; butter (Lima) beans; black beans; pinto beans; haricot (white) beans; avocados; raisins; kidney beans; chard; prune juice; parsnips; split peas; blackstrap molasses; dates; potatoes; kohlrabi; peas; Brussels sprouts and nectarines.

Salt in cooking water: By adding salt to the cooking water, you are not only adding sodium, but minerals contained within the foods are actually depleted, for example, salt added to the cooking water of spinach reduces the iron content by 50 per cent compared to a 19 per cent loss when cooked without salt. Lemon juice added to the cooking water prevents the vegetables from losing their colour.

Hidden sodium: There are huge amounts of sodium in snack and convenience foods and drinks. In a litre of *Vichy* water there is 3.630g of bicarbonate of soda, but in *Perrier* water there is only 0.024mg of sodium and *Contrexville* water contains an extremely low amount of 0.002mg.

Bottled sauces and flavourings contain huge amounts of sodium:

	per 100g
Table salt	38850 mg
Block salt	38700 mg
Baking powder	11800 mg
Oxo cubes	10300 mg
Curry powder	4800 mg
Barley miso (barley & soyabean)	4600 mg
Genmai miso (rice miso)	4600 mg

Hatcho miso (soyabean miso)	4100 mg
Tamari	3600 mg
Olives in brine	2250 mg
Sweet pickle	1700 mg
Shoyu	1300 mg
Picalilli	1200 mg
Tomato ketchup	1120 mg
Cocoa powder	950 mg
Baked beans	480 mg
Peanuts, roasted and salted	440 mg
Peanut butter	350 mg
Peas, processed	330 mg
Sweetcorn, tinned	310 mg
Carrots, tinned	280 mg
Peas, tinned	230 mg

How Can Sodium Content be Reduced?

There are many ways of reducing the sodium content of meals, but remember it is more effective and long term if you do it slowly.

Throughout this book there are many suggestions for producing tasty food, where the addition of salt is not necessary. When buying food, look for wording on the sides of packaging such as: monosodium glutamate; Na; soda; salt; sodium bicarbonate; baking soda; as these all refer to salt or sodium.

Fresh vegetables: By using fresh vegetables, the potassium content of the meal is considerably increased and decreases the sodium content, for example:

	mg. per 100g
Carrots, tinned	280
fresh, cooked, old	50
fresh, cooked, young	23
Peas, processed	330
tinned	230
fresh, cooked	Trace

Sweetcorn, tinned	310
fresh, cooked	1
Beetroot, pickled	379
fresh, cooked	64

Most tinned foods have a high content of sodium and you should avoid them at all times. It is quite easy to buy tinned tomatoes in tomato sauce in preference to those tinned in brine. The names to look for on labels are:

Baking powder
Sodium bicarbonate
Sodium benzoate E211   all of these are
Monosodium glutamate   sodium-based additives
Sodium additives

Baking Powder: Sodium kills Vitamin B in food so cakes with a pinch of salt and commercial baking powder as a rising agent should be avoided. In the book we use a home-made potassium-based baking powder which has a very low sodium content.

Potassium Baking Powder

Cream of tartar
Potassium bicarbonate
Arrowroot

Mix equal quantities of these ingredients together and use in recipes as you would use commercial baking powder. This baking powder keeps very well in a screw-top jar.

Butter and Spreads: Purely by using unsalted butter instead of salted butter.

		Sodium Content
4 oz (100g/½ cupful) Salted butter	=	870 mg
4 oz (100g/½ cupful) Margarine	=	690 mg
4 oz (100g/½ cupful) Unsalted butter	=	7 mg
4 oz (100g/1 cupful) Peanut butter	=	350 mg

Cheese: The various cheeses contain differing amounts of sodium, a general rule being the stronger tasting and harder the cheese, the more sodium it contains.

	mg. per 100g
Danish Blue	1420
Camembert	1410
Processed cheese	1360
Cheese spread	1170
Stilton	1150
Edam	980
Parmesan	760
Cottage cheese	450
Cream cheese	300
Yogurt cheese	152 approx.

It is very rare that a sodium deficiency ever occurs, since the daily requirement is so low. In Britain the average daily consumption of sodium is 2½-3 teaspoonsful, compared to a maximum recommended daily intake of 1½ teaspoonsful and an ideal ½ teaspoonful as recommended by health authorities. Even people on a vegetarian diet obtain sufficient sodium from foods without having to add it.

How to Stop Shaking the Salt
Some people actually pick up the salt pot before they have even tasted the food. Australian researchers found that by placing the salt cellar out of reach, less people are likely to use it. I think it is very important that people distinguish the need for salt as being psychological rather than nutritional. To break habits and tastes of a lifetime is not easy. In this book in place of table salt, I have given you recipes for Gomasio (page 21) and Eastern Sprinkle (page 19) both lower-sodium condiments.

Flavouring is brought about by the use of herbs, spices, fruit juice, sea vegetables, seaweed water, sesame seeds, oats, vegetables and marinades.

I hope, with its variety of ideas, that this book will enable you to be 'below the salt' and 'higher in health'.

Types of Salt

Salt is usually a natural product obtained from the land and the sea.

Table salt: This is obtained from land where water is pumped into underground salt mines. This produces a brine. To make salt the brine is refined to remove the trace minerals, then steam heated under great pressure to 1200°F (631.1°C) and 'flash cooled' to produce instant crystallization. Minerals lost in refining are never replaced. For salt to be free-running, anti-caking additives in the form of magnesium carbonate, phosphate of lime, starch or sodium hexanoferrate II are added.

Rock Salt: Rock salt is the same as sea salt in that it retains its mineral content but is often sold in a large crystal form. Rock salt is higher in sodium chloride than sea salt.

Crystal Salt: Crystal salt can be obtained from the sea or land salt and is pure salt. French cooks are very keen on using freshly ground crystal salt as it is proported to have a superior flavour.

Sea Salt: Sea salt is obtained from evaporating sea water. After the sea salt has been extracted it leaves a mineral rich liquor which is called 'nigari' or 'bitterns' (this is used to solidify tofu in tofu making). Sea salt is a natural product often rich in iodine and does not usually contain additives. It has a high sodium content and should be treated like gold dust in cooking! Many manufacturers are more and more aware of the pollution in the sea and are actually mining sea salt from rock where the prehistoric seas covered the earth. One gallon (4 litres/1.2 U.S. gallons) of sea water yields 4 ounces (100g) of sea salt. When dry, sea salt consists of:

	per cent
Sodium chloride	77.8
Magnesium chloride	9.5
Magnesium sulphate	6.6
Calcium sulphate	3.4
Potassium chloride	2.1
Magnesium bromide	0.2
Trace elements and impurities	0.4

Iodised Salt: Generally this consists of table salt with added potassium iodide. It is not to be confused with true salt substitutes which do not usually contain any sodium chloride. Salt substitutes are easily found in health food shops but I suggest you would be better off buying a variety of herbs, spices and natural extracts.

Miso: This is a purée made from the fermentation of soya beans, grain and salt.

Sodium content of miso:

	per cent	per 100g
Barley miso (Mugi miso)	13	4600 mg
Soya bean miso (Hatcho miso)	11.2	4100 mg
Rice miso (Genmai miso)	13	4600 mg
Tamari (liquid soya bean miso)	11.3	3600 mg

Miso high in salt tends to be low in carbohydrate and miso low in salt tends to be high in carbohydrate. All of the miso's have different properties in cooking. The barley miso is sweeter than rice miso and has a high protein content (13 per cent) with a low carbohydrate content (21 per cent). Soya bean, or hatcho, miso is very dark in colour, the liquid form of this miso is called tamari. (To test for genuine tamari and shoyu shake the bottle and bubbles will form and hold as opposed to the disappearing bubbles on commercial soya sauces made with sugar and monosodium glutamate.) Tamari is well known in cooking for its strong flavour, high salt taste containing less sodium chloride for the same salty flavour than shoyu. I do not recommend the use of shoyu or tamari on a no sodium chloride (salt) diet, but stress to the reader, if you have to use salt in cooking at any time, of all the sodium chloride flavourings on the market tamari would be the best.

Before You Start to Cook
In replacing salt and making tasty food I find it essential to prepare ingredients, which saves a great deal of time and frustration!

For example, it was very useful to mix a jar of cumin and coriander powder in equal quantities, so where a recipe called for equal quantities I just had to get it from one container. In the ethnic shops I found an excellent tin for spices called a *masala* tin. It holds seven spices in one tin which is extremely useful. It meant filling the tin every week or so but saved cleaning seven spice jars every time I cooked. If you buy more than one tin make sure that you purchase two different sizes as they are all made of stainless steel and there is nothing more frustrating than getting out the wrong tin!

Herbs play an essential part in salt-free cooking, and to make sure I have enough herbs throughout the winter I plant the summer hanging baskets with herb plants. They can be kept in porches or inside sheds, hung in the window, laundry areas or even in the kitchen provided they have sufficient light.

I keep stored dried herbs in brown beer bottles with cork stoppers as direct sunlight reduces the flavour of the herbs considerably.

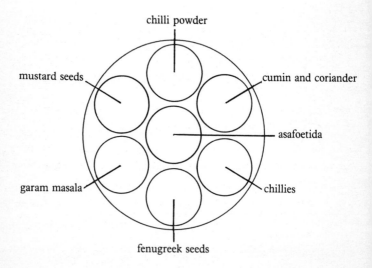

1.

LOW-SALT 'SPRINKLES', SOUPS AND SAUCES

'EASTERN SPRINKLE'

This is made with dried leaves, sea vegetables and dried miso soup and has the appearance of pepper. The nori, like all sea vegetables is rich in minerals, and the shiso is a fragrant herb. These two mixed with the naturally fermented and dried miso brings down the sodium content of the condiment.

Imperial (Metric)	American
1 oz (25g) shiso leaves (beefsteak plant)	1 ounce shiso leaves (beefsteak plant)
2 oz (50g) nori (sheet sea vegetable)	2 ounces nori (sheet sea vegetable)
½ oz (15g) miso soup (dried)	½ ounce miso soup (dried)

1. The shiso leaves are usually bought ground. Roast the nori in a grill, open flame or oven. When it is roasted you can grind it very fine.

2. Mix all of the ingredients together and place in a salt cellar.

OATS AND SESAME

Imperial (Metric)
4 oz (100g) sesame seeds
2 oz (50g) oats
½ oz (15g) sea salt

American
¾ cupful sesame seeds
½ cupful oats
½ ounce sea salt

1. Roast the oats and sesame seeds together and grind with the salt.
    The oats lighten the colour of the salt and make it look more
    like table salt.

Note: None of these salts are suitable for people on a sodium free
diet, but may be useful in those initial stages of cutting salt down
in the diet. All of the recipes in this book are salt free, allowing the
individual to choose if they want to add salt and offering condiments
that we have just mentioned for the 'shakers'.

GOMASIO

Shaking salt can be habit forming and gomasio or sesame seed salt is often a very good introduction to reducing salt. It is tasty and pleasant.

Imperial (Metric)
4 oz (100g) sesame seeds
½ oz (15g) sea salt

American
¾ cupful sesame seeds
½ ounce sea salt

1. Roast the sesame seeds in a frying pan with no oil, or in an oven. You can tell when they are cooked because they give off a lovely aroma and they begin to pop; make sure you have a lid at hand or they will be all over the cooker.

2. When the seeds are roasted grind them and the salt together in a coffee grinder or *surabachi* (grinding bowl). As you become more and more used to it you can decrease the salt content and increase the sesame seed content.

'SPRINKLE'

General flavouring for vegetable dishes, soups and sauces or just use as a sprinkle in a pepper pot.

Imperial (Metric)	American
3 oz (75g) marjoram	3 ounces marjoram
1 oz (25g) oregano	1 ounce oregano
2 oz (50g) thyme	2 ounces thyme
1 teaspoonful savory	1 teaspoonful savory
1 teaspoonful cayenne pepper	1 teaspoonful cayenne pepper
1 oz (15g) ground bay leaves	1 ounce ground bay leaves
½ teaspoonful ground mace	½ teaspoonful ground mace
½ teaspoonful nutmeg	½ teaspoonful nutmeg
½ teaspoonful ground ginger	½ teaspoonful ground ginger

1.   Mix all the ingredients together. Store in a screw-top jar.

SALTY JUICES

Imperial (Metric)
1 tablespoonful tamarind
1 pint (500ml) water

American
1 tablespoonful tamarind
2²/₃ cupsful water

1. Leave the tamarind to soak for an hour in half the water. Bits of dirt and straw will rise to the surface. Discard the soaking water and rinse the tamarind.

2. Place the rest of the water in a saucepan with the tamarind and boil until the tamarind is soft.

3. Use sparingly as a salting agent, as if over-used, like any potassium product it can taste bitter.

GHEE

A combination of ghee and spice can be used as a seasoning agent called *Tharka*.

Ghee can be more convenient in cooking than unprocessed butter as it will not burn or 'scorch' when used for sautéing. Butter is not pure fat, it also contains water and milk solids which turn black when used in cooking. To make ghee, the water and milk solids have to be separated and strained off.

Imperial (Metric)
½ lb (220g) unsalted butter

American
1 cupful unsalted butter

1. Place the unsalted butter in a saucepan and heat slowly. The water will evaporate with the gentle heating and the milk solids will be left. You will know this has taken place when the 'sound' changes, there will be a positive sizzling and the bubbling will stop.

2. Skim the sediment off the top and there will be a golden sediment on the bottom of the pan. At this point the ghee is ready and the temperature will begin to rise quickly, so remove the pan from the heat.

3. Strain through muslin or a nylon coffee filter, into a *glass* container: don't forget hot fat can melt plastic containers.

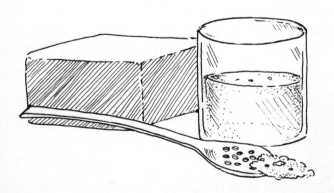

EMPORIUM SOUP

Imperial (Metric)	American
2 oz (50g) red kidney beans	¼ cupful red kidney beans
½ lb (200g) onions	8 ounces onions
½ lb (200g) tomatoes	8 ounces tomatoes
2 oz (50g) carrots	2 ounces carrots
3 garlic cloves	3 garlic cloves
1 piece kombu	1 piece kombu
1 chopped chilli	1 chopped chili
1 oz (25g) pot barley	2 tablespoonsful pot barley
1 oz (25g) wholemeal pasta shapes	½ cupful wholemeal pasta shapes
2 teaspoonsful 'Sprinkle'	2 teaspoonsful 'Sprinkle'
(see page 22)	(see page 22)

1. Soak the kidney beans.

2. Peel and chop the onions.

3. Skin the tomatoes by placing in boiling water.

4. Grate the carrot.

5. Peel and chop the garlic.

6. Soak the kombu in 1½ pints (850ml/3¾ cupsful) water.

7. Chop the chilli very finely and remove the seeds.

8. Cook the kidney beans, barley, pasta and the kombu in the soaking water from the kombu.

9. When the beans can be pressed between the thumb and middle finger, add the onions, tomatoes, grated carrot, chopped garlic, 'Sprinkle' and chopped chilli.

10. Leave the mixture to cool and chill for 10 hours or overnight. Heat and serve.

LENTIL SOUP

Imperial (Metric)
6 oz (150g) split lentils
4 tomatoes
1 tablespoonful sesame seed oil
1 tablespoonful mustard seeds
1 teaspoonful cumin powder
1 teaspoonful coriander
½ teaspoonful crushed cloves
3 limdo leaves (curry leaves)
1 oz (25g) raisins
1 tablespoonful cashew nuts
2 tablespoonsful concentrated apple
   juice

American
¾ cupful split lentils
4 tomatoes
1 tablespoonful sesame seed oil
1 tablespoonful mustard seeds
1 teaspoonful cumin powder
1 teaspoonful coriander
½ teaspoonful crushed cloves
3 limdo leaves (curry leaves)
2 tablespoonsful raisins
1 tablespoonful cashew nuts
2 tablespoonsful concentrated apple
   juice

1. Cook the lentils in 2 pints of water.

2. Slice the tomatoes.

3. Heat the oil and add the mustard seeds.

4. Add cumin, coriander, cloves, limdo leaves and cooked lentils with water. Bring to the boil and simmer.

5. Add the raisins, cashew nuts and sliced tomatoes.

6. Add apple juice just before serving.

TOMATO SOUP

Imperial (Metric)
2 lb (800g) fresh tomatoes
1 oz (25g) fresh parsley
1 tablespoonful fennel seeds
1 teaspoonful kelp powder

American
2 pounds fresh tomatoes
1 ounce fresh parsley
1 tablespoonful fennel seeds
1 teaspoonful kelp powder

1. Cut the tomatoes in half, drain and reserve the juice.

2. Wash and chop the parsley.

3. Cook the tomatoes with the fennel seeds in ½ pint (285ml/1⅓ cupsful) water.

4. When soft, add the kelp powder and tomato juice and liquidize the mixture.

5. Serve with chopped parsley and Pine and Cumin Bread (page 104).

TOFU MAYONNAISE

Imperial (Metric)	American
6 oz (150g) silken tofu	¾ cupful silken tofu
2 tablespoonsful tamarind water	2 tablespoonsful tamarind water
1 teaspoonful mustard seeds	1 teaspoonful mustard seeds
1 teaspoonful tahini	1 teaspoonful tahini
1 teaspoonful olive oil	1 teaspoonful olive oil
½ teaspoonful masala dal or curry powder	½ teaspoonful masala dal or curry powder
1 oz (25g) cashew nuts (optional)	3 tablespoonsful cashew nuts (optional)
1 tablespoonful lemon juice	1 tablespoonful lemon juice

1. Liquidize all the ingredients together, adding water slowly to make a thick smooth mayonnaise.

Variation:
By adding 2 tablespoonsful of tomato sauce, this makes a nicely flavoured mayonnaise to use with rice salads.

CHILLI SAUCE

Imperial (Metric)	American
6 oz (150g) dried red kidney beans	1 cupful dried red kidney beans
1 lb (400g) tomatoes	1 pound tomatoes
1 bunch spring onions	1 bunch scallions
1 small chilli (the smaller the chilli, the hotter the flavour)	1 small chili (the smaller the chili, the hotter the flavour)
1 medium potato (old potatoes, not new)	1 medium potato (old potatoes, not new)
1 tablespoonful cold-pressed sesame oil	1 tablespoonful cold-pressed sesame oil
¼ teaspoonful freshly ground black pepper	¼ teaspoonful freshly ground black pepper
1 teaspoonful kelp	1 teaspoonful kelp
4 oz (100g) fresh coriander	4 ounces cilantro

1. Wash and soak red kidney beans overnight.

2. Peel the tomatoes by placing them in a bowl of hot water for a few seconds until the skin slips off easily.

3. Wash and chop the spring onions (scallions) into 2-inch (5cm) pieces.

4. Wash and chop the chilli very finely.

5. Clean and grate the potato.

6. Cook the red kidney beans for approximately 30 minutes in a pressure cooker or 1½ hours in a saucepan with a tightly-fitting lid . To test whether they are cooked, squeeze one between the thumb and middle finger.

7. Sauté the spring onions (scallions) and chilli in the oil. Add the kidney beans, when cooked, and the grated potato. Turn off the heat and place a lid on the pan — otherwise they will burn.

8. Liquidize the fresh tomatoes and add to the bean mixture.

9. Simmer the mixture until the potato becomes part of the sauce and the liquid has been simmered off the tomatoes, making it thicker.

10. Add the pepper and kelp and taste the mixture at this stage. If it is not hot enough add more very finely chopped chilli.

11. Serve hot or cold with fresh coriander (cilantro) on the top. Eat with Garlic Bread and an apple salad or brown rice with a salad of grapes and apples.

BEAN SAUCE

Imperial (Metric)	American
6 oz (150g) aduki beans	¾ cupful aduki beans
1 apple	1 apple
3 cloves garlic	3 cloves garlic
1 lb (400g) fresh tomatoes	1 pound fresh tomatoes
1 tablespoonful olive oil	1 tablespoonful olive oil
½ teaspoonful celery seeds	½ teaspoonful celery seeds
1 tablespoonful fresh or ½ tablespoonful dried lovage	1 tablespoonful fresh or ½ tablespoonful dried lovage

1. Soak the aduki beans for approximately 3 hours in cold water.

2. Grate the apple. Peel the garlic and chop very finely. Clean the tomatoes and cut into small pieces.

3. Cook the aduki beans for approximately 20 minutes in ¾ pint (425ml/2 cupsful) water in a pressure cooker until they are reduced to a thick purée. (If you cook the beans in a saucepan, keep checking that they do not burn.)

4. Sauté the garlic in the olive oil.

5. Add the celery seeds, lovage, apple and tomatoes and cook till tender.

6. Mix the aduki beans and sautéed garlic mixture together.

7. Simmer the sauce and serve hot — for a creamy sauce add 4 fl oz (120ml/½ cupful) yogurt or 4 oz (100g/½ cupful) silken tofu.

TOMATO SAUCE

Imperial (Metric)	American
3 lbs (1.2 kilos) tomatoes	3 pounds tomatoes
1/3 cupful wine vinegar	1/2 cupful wine vinegar
1/3 cupful honey *or* malt	1/2 cupful honey *or* malt
1 pinch grated nutmeg	1 pinch grated nutmeg
1 teaspoonful cloves	1 teaspoonful cloves
2 teaspoonsful kelp	2 teaspoonsful kelp

1. Skin the tomatoes by dipping into hot water for a few seconds, until the skin can be slipped off.

2. Slice the tomatoes and squeeze out the juice.

3. Place all ingredients except the kelp together in a saucepan and cook over a very low heat for approximately 1 hour.

4. Just before serving add the 2 teaspoonsful of kelp.

5. Serve hot or cold. Can be stored in a glass jar in the refrigerator.

CUCUMBER AND ONION CHUTNEY

Imperial (Metric)	American
½ cucumber	½ cucumber
1 large Spanish onion	1 large Spanish onion
4 fl oz (120ml) natural yogurt	½ cupful plain yogurt
1 teaspoonful dill	1 teaspoonful dill
¼ teaspoonful chilli powder	¼ teaspoonful chili powder
1 teaspoonful malt	1 teaspoonful malt
Fresh coriander to garnish	Fresh cilantro to garnish

1. Chop the cucumber into cubes and place on a tea towel or kitchen towel to dry.

2. Chop the onion very finely.

3. Mix all the ingredients together. Take care that the cucumber is quite dry, be careful not to squeeze more liquid out of it as you mix.

4. Chill and serve garnished with chopped fresh coriander (cilantro).

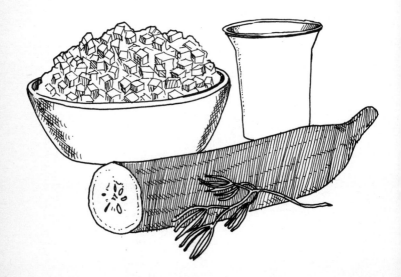

BANANA, ONION AND TOMATO CHUTNEY

Imperial (Metric)
1 large onion
1 lb (400g) tomatoes
2 bananas

American
1 large onion
1 pound tomatoes
2 bananas

1. Chop the onions very finely.

2. Wash, slice and cube tomatoes.

3. Peel and cube the bananas.

4. Place all of the ingredients in a bowl and mix well together. If left to stand for long enough, the banana disintegrates and becomes a thick binding liquid.

Note: Onions can be replaced in this recipe by very finely chopped leeks. It is also an excellent way of using up green tomatoes and they give it a good colour.

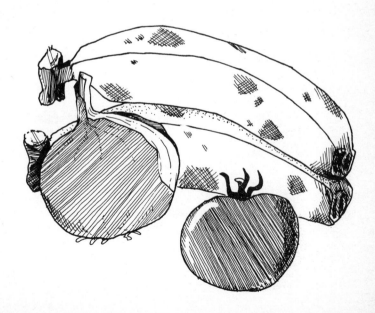

COCONUT CHUTNEY

Imperial (Metric)
1 teaspoonful garam masala
½ teaspoonful cinnamon
½ teaspoonful cumin
1 teaspoonful ground coriander
4 oz (100g) grated coconut
4 fl oz (120ml) natural yogurt

American
1 teaspoonful garam masala (curry powder)
½ teaspoonful cinnamon
½ teaspoonful cumin
1 teaspoonful ground coriander
1⅓ cupsful grated coconut
½ cupful plain yogurt

1. Mix all of the ingredients together and serve — this chutney is lovely with bean dishes.

APPLE CRUNCH SAUCE

Imperial (Metric)
1 lb (400g) sour cooking apples
1 tablespoonful cider vinegar
1 tablespoonful cumin powder
1 tablespoonful ground coriander
3 tablespoonsful ground mustard
  seeds
2 tablespoonsful cold-pressed
  safflower oil
2 tablespoonsful concentrated apple
  juice

American
1 pound sour cooking apples
1 tablespoonful cider vinegar
1 tablespoonful cumin powder
1 tablespoonful ground coriander
3 tablespoonsful ground mustard
  seeds
2 tablespoonsful cold-pressed
  safflower oil
2 tablespoonsful concentrated apple
  juice

1. Wash the apples in water with cider vinegar — this helps to remove any wax and pesticide spray.

2. Core the apples and slice into small pieces.

3. Mix the cumin, coriander, mustard seeds, oil and apple juice together.

4. Add the apples and mix well together. Serve with Fenugreek Pancakes (page 56) or Chapatis (page 50).

2.

MAIN COURSES

CHESTNUT ROAST

Imperial (Metric)	American
4 oz (100g) onions	4 ounces onions
1 clove garlic	1 clove garlic
1 green pepper	1 green pepper
6 oz (150g) chestnuts	6 ounces chestnuts
6 oz (150g) cashew nuts	1¼ cupsful cashew nuts
4 oz (100g) cranberries	1 cupful cranberries
1 teaspoonful fresh oregano	1 teaspoonful fresh oregano
1 tablespoonful cold-pressed sesame oil	1 tablespoonful cold-pressed sesame oil
4 oz (100g) wholemeal breadcrumbs	2 cupsful wholewheat breadcrumbs
1 oz (25g) ground sesame seeds	¼ cupful ground sesame seeds
4 oz (100g) sugar-free raspberry jam	⅓ cupful sugar-free raspberry jam

1. Finely chop the onion, garlic and green pepper.

2. Roast the chestnuts at 400°F/200°C (Gas Mark 6). Pierce every chestnut except one because when that one bursts or bangs in the oven then the rest are roasted and ready to be peeled. Peel and cut into small pieces.

3. Chop the cashew nuts into small pieces.

4. Stew the cranberries in enough water to cover them.

5. Sauté the garlic, pepper, oregano and onions in the oil.

6. Mix together the nuts, breadcrumbs, sautéed vegetables and sesame seeds.

7. Mix the cranberries with the raspberry jam.

8. Oil a 2 pound (1 kilo) loaf tin and line it. Oil the lining paper.

9. Place a 1-inch (2.5cm) layer of chestnut mixture in the tin.

10. Spread with ¼-inch (5mm) cranberry sauce, repeat this once more and finish with nut mixture to cover the cranberry sauce.

11. Bake at 300°F/150°C (Gas Mark 2) for 45 minutes. Serve with puréed sprouts as a sauce.

LADIES FINGERS

Imperial (Metric)	American
2 tablespoonsful cold-pressed sesame seed oil	2 tablespoonsful cold-pressed sesame seed oil
1 tablespoonful mustard seeds	1 tablespoonful mustard seeds
2 cloves garlic	2 cloves garlic
1-inch (2.5cm) cube fresh ginger	1-inch cube fresh ginger
1 tablespoonful coriander and cumin, mixed	1 tablespoonful coriander and cumin, mixed
1 lb (400g) okra	1 pound okra
1 cup Tomato Sauce (page 31)	1¼ cupsful Tomato Sauce (page 31)

1. When choosing the okra make sure they are tender. Wash and cut off the tops.

2. Grate the ginger.

3. Peel and chop the garlic very finely.

4. Heat the oil in a deep pan with a well-fitting lid.

5. Add the mustard seeds, turn off the heat, put on the saucepan lid and you will hear the seeds pop.

6. Once the popping has stopped, add the garlic, ginger and cumin/coriander powder. Mix well.

7. Add the okra and simmer gently in the spiced oil for 4 minutes. Turn off the heat and leave to steam with the lid on the saucepan until tender (approximately 25 minutes.)

8. Add the Tomato Sauce and serve hot or cold with Chapatis (page 50) and yogurt.

LENTIL QUICHE

Imperial (Metric)	American
4 oz (100g) onions	4 ounces onions
1 teaspoonful kelp powder	1 teaspoonful kelp powder
1 teaspoonful fresh hyssop or ½ teaspoonful dried hyssop	1 teaspoonful fresh hyssop or ½ teaspoonful dried hyssop
1 teaspoonful fresh winter or summer savory or ½ teaspoonful dried	1 teaspoonful fresh winter or summer savory or ½ teaspoonful dried
3 cloves garlic	3 cloves garlic
1 teaspoonful cayenne pepper	1 teaspoonful cayenne pepper
½ pint (285ml) Tomato Sauce (page 31) or tomato juice	1⅓ cupsful Tomato Sauce (page 31) or tomato juice
½ lb (200g) Salt-free Pastry (page 108)	8 ounces Salt-free Pastry (page 108)
4 oz (100g) cooked lentils	4 oz (100g) cooked lentils
1 egg or 2 oz (50g) tofu	1 egg or ¼ cupful tofu

1. Peel and roughly chop the onions.

2. Liquidize the onions, kelp powder, hyssop, savoury, garlic and cayenne pepper in the Tomato Sauce or juice.

3. If using tofu instead of an egg, liquidize the tofu with enough water to make a thick sauce-like consistency.

4. Oil a 10-inch (25cm) quiche dish.

5. Roll out the pastry between two pieces of greaseproof paper. To line the quiche dish, remove the top piece of greaseproof, roll the pastry up with the underneath piece (like a Swiss-roll), turn it over and unroll into the quiche dish.

6. Mix the lentils, liquidized tomato and onion together and simmer until thick. Take care that it does not stick. Cool.

7. Add the egg or tofu, place in the quiche dish and bake at 400°F/200°C (Gas Mark 6) for approximately 30 minutes or until filling is set. Serve with lettuce and orange salad.

COTTAGE CHEESE AND ONION QUICHE

Imperial (Metric)	American
½ lb (200g) Salt-free Pastry (page 108)	8 ounces Salt-free Pastry (page 108)
4 oz (100g) onions	4 oz (100g) onions
1 clove garlic	1 clove garlic
2 eggs	2 eggs
4 fl oz (120ml) natural yogurt	½ cupful plain yogurt
1 teaspoonful fresh or ½ teaspoonful dried basil	1 teaspoonful fresh or ½ teaspoonful dried basil
½ lb (200g) low-fat cottage cheese	1 cupful low-fat cottage cheese
4 oz (100g) mushrooms	2 cupsful mushrooms

1. Line an oiled 10-inch (25cm) quiche tin with the pastry.

2. Peel and cut onions into quarters.

3. Peel the garlic.

4. Liquidize the eggs, yogurt, basil, onions and garlic.

5. When the eggs are liquidized mix in the low-fat cottage cheese.

6. Wipe and slice the mushrooms.

7. Oil the pastry case lightly or brush with egg white to stop the egg mixture soaking into it.

8. Place the egg and cheese mixture into the quiche case. Add the sliced mushrooms.

9. Bake at 350°F/180°C (Gas Mark 4) for approximately 35 minutes until set.

10. Serve hot, or cool by placing the quiche dish on a cooling rack (this stops the pastry going soggy).

TOMATO PASTIES

Imperial (Metric)	American
4 oz (100g) onions	4 ounces onions
14 oz (400g) tin tomatoes (unsalted)	14 ounce can tomatoes (unsalted)
2 cloves garlic	2 cloves garlic
1 teaspoonful ground rosemary	1 teaspoonful ground rosemary
½ lb (200g) Salt-free Pastry (page 108)	8 ounces Salt-free Pastry (page 108)

1. Peel and chop the onions.

2. Place the tomatoes in a liquidizer, add the garlic and onions.

3. Add the ground rosemary and boil the mixture until reduced by one third.

4. Oil a baking tray.

5. Preheat the oven to 400°F/200°C (Gas Mark 6).

6. Roll out the pastry and cut into 6-inch (15cm) rounds.

7. Place some tomato mixture in the middle of each round.

8. Fold over and seal the edges of the pastry with water.

9. Place the pasties on a flat baking sheet and cook for 20 minutes.

10. Serve hot with salad and chutney or cold in lunch boxes.

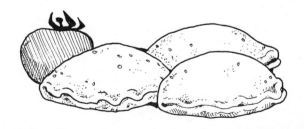

BAKED BEANS

Imperial (Metric)	American
½ lb (200g) haricot beans	1 cupful navy beans
6 oz (150g) onions	6 ounces onions
1 tablespoonful kelp	1 tablespoonful kelp
1 pint (500ml) tomato juice	2½ cupsful tomato juice
2 oz (50g) malt	2 tablespoonsful malt

1. Soak the haricot (navy) beans in cold water for 4 hours.

2. Peel the onions and chop roughly.

3. Liquidize the kelp, onions and tomato juice together.

4. Cook the haricot (navy) beans until you can squeeze them between the middle finger and thumb (approximately 30 minutes in a pressure cooker or 1¼ hours in a saucepan).

5. When the beans are cooked, place in a dish with the tomato sauce and malt and bake them at 300°F/150°C (Gas Mark 2) for approximately 35 minutes.

SPINACH SOUFFLÉ

Imperial (Metric)	American
1 lb (400g) spinach	1 pound spinach
2 teaspoonsful fresh *or* 1 teaspoonful dried thyme	2 teaspoonsful fresh *or* 1 teaspoonful dried thyme
2 teaspoonsful fresh *or* 1 teaspoonful dried oregano	2 teaspoonsful fresh *or* 1 teaspoonful dried oregano
½ lb (200g) silken tofu	1 cupful silken tofu
1 teaspoonful kelp powder	1 teaspoonful kelp powder
1 tablespoonful oil *or* ghee	1 tablespoonful oil *or* ghee
4 egg whites	4 egg whites
½ teaspoonful freshly ground black pepper	½ teaspoonful freshly ground black pepper

1. Wash and chop the spinach very finely.

2. Wash and chop the thyme and oregano.

3. Make sauce by liquidizing the silken tofu with the kelp powder and pepper in 6 tablespoonsful water.

4. Sauté the spinach in oil or ghee.

5. Add spinach to the tofu sauce and leave to cool.

6. Whisk the egg whites.

7. Mix the spinach and tofu sauce with the egg whites, season with black pepper and place in an oiled soufflé dish.

8. Bake at 375°F/190°C (Gas Mark 5) for 30-35 minutes. Serve immediately with a rice salad and Melon Tomato and Cucumber Salad (page 75).

CAULIFLOWER CURRY

Imperial (Metric)	American
1 cauliflower	1 cauliflower
½ lb (200g) tomatoes	8 ounces tomatoes
1 piece kombu (sea vegetable)	1 piece kombu (sea vegetable)
4 oz (100g) potatoes	4 ounces potatoes
1 small chilli (more if you want it really hot)	1 small chili (more if you want it really hot)
2 cloves garlic	2 cloves garlic
2 tablespoonsful cold-pressed sunflower oil	2 tablespoonsful cold-pressed sunflower oil
1 teaspoonful mustard seeds (black)	1 teaspoonful mustard seeds (black)
1 teaspoonful cumin seeds	1 teaspoonful cumin seeds
1 tablespoonful coriander and cumin powder, mixed	1 tablespoonful coriander and cumin powder, mixed
Pinch of asafoetida	Pinch of asafoetida
4 oz (100g) onions	4 ounces onions
1 teaspoonful turmeric	1 teaspoonful turmeric

1. Clean the cauliflower and break into florets, cut the stalk into ½-inch (1cm) cubes.

2. Clean and slice the tomatoes.

3. Soak the kambu in ½ pint (285ml) water.

4. Scrub and slice the potato very finely.

5. Chop the chilli very finely with the garlic.

6. Heat the oil and add the black mustard seeds. When they have popped, add the cumin seeds, garlic, chilli, cumin and coriander powder and asafoetida.

7. Chop the onions. Add the onions and cauliflower, turn the heat down low and put a lid on the pan. Let the food steam gently.

8. When the vegetables have steamed for 5 minutes, add the liquid from the kombu, tomatoes, potatoes and turmeric. Cook the curry till the potato has disintegrated and become part of the sauce.

9. Once the cauliflower is tender, but not soggy, the curry is ready.

NUT RISSOLES

Imperial (Metric)	**American**
4 oz (100g) Brazil nuts	1 cupful Brazil nuts
3 oz (75g) cooked chick peas	½ cupful cooked garbanzo beans
2 cloves garlic	2 cloves garlic
3 tablespoonsful tomato purée	3 tablespoonsful tomato paste
2 tablespoonsful tahini	2 tablespoonsful tahini
1 oz (30g) fresh *or* ½ oz (12g) dried sage, finely chopped	1 ounce fresh *or* ½ ounce dried sage, finely chopped

1. Grind the Brazil nuts.

2. Mash the chick peas (garbanzo beans).

3. Liquidize the garlic in the tomato purée.

4. Mix all the ingredients together and shape into rissoles. Leave to stand in the fridge for 1 hour.

5. Shallow fry or grill to serve. Serve with Apple Crunch Sauce (page 35) and jacket potatoes.

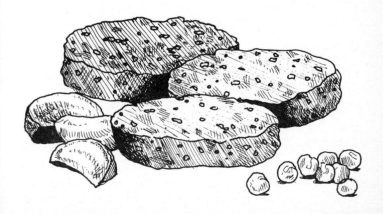

RICE BALLS

Imperial (Metric)	American
6 oz (150g) brown rice	1 cupful brown rice
2 bunches spring onions	2 bunches scallions
1 teaspoonful fresh *or* ½ teaspoonful dried basil	1 teaspoonful fresh *or* ½ teaspoonful dried basil
1 teaspoonful fresh parsley	1 teaspoonful fresh parsley
1 teaspoonful fresh celery leaves	1 teaspoonful fresh celery leaves
2 tablespoonsful white wine *or* rice vinegar *or* juice of ½ lemon	2 tablespoonsful white wine *or* rice vinegar *or* juice of ½ lemon
½ lb (200g) gram flour	1½ cupsful gram flour
1 tablespoonful garam masala	1 tablespoonful garam masala (curry powder)
1 tablespoonful baking powder	1 tablespoonful baking powder
Oil for deep frying	Oil for deep frying

1. Wash and cook the rice in twice its volume of water, do not stir as it cooks from the bottom up and the top grains should steam. Always use a pan with a tightly fitting lid.

2. Clean and chop the spring onions (scallions), basil, parsley and celery leaves.

3. Mix together 1 tablespoonful garam masala, baking powder and gram flour.

4. When the rice is cooked, pound it with a pestle or potato masher until it becomes broken down and the grains are flattened.

5. Mix the white wine, herbs and spring onions (scallions) in with the rice and shape into balls. The smaller the ball the nicer they look.

6. Make a batter by mixing the gram flour to a coating consistency with water.

7. Heat the oil. When the oil is heated add 1 tablespoonful of warm oil to the batter and mix well.

8. Drop a tiny amount of the batter into the oil and if it rises to the surface the oil is ready. Make sure the oil never smokes but that it is hot before the food is put in it.

9. Dip the rice balls in the batter and deep fry. Serve the rice balls with Banana, Onion and Tomato Chutney (page 33) and green salad.

RICE RING

Imperial (Metric)	American
2 oz (50g) cashew nuts	½ cupful cashew nuts
2 oz (50g) fresh ginger	2 ounces fresh ginger
4 oz (100g) fresh coriander	4 ounces cilantro
4 oz (100g) fresh parsley	4 ounces fresh parsley
½ lb (200g) mushrooms	4 cupsful mushrooms
6 oz (150g) arame (sea vegetable)	6 ounces arame (sea vegetable)
4 oz (100g) red peppers	4 ounces red peppers
4 oz (100g) green peppers	4 ounces green peppers
½ lb (200g) tofu	1 cupful tofu
4 fl oz (120ml) yogurt	½ cupful yogurt
2 oz (50g) sunflower seeds	½ cupful sunflower seeds
4 oz (100g) pine nuts	1 cupful pine nuts
14 oz (400g) cooked brown rice	2⅓ cupsful cooked brown rice

1. Grind the cashew nuts until fine. Grate the ginger. Chop the coriander (cilantro) and parsley very finely. Clean and chop the mushrooms finely.

2. Soak the arame in ½ pint (285ml/1⅓ cupsful) water.

3. Wash and slice the peppers into rings.

4. Liquidize the tofu, yogurt, ginger, seeds and nuts together.

5. Mix together brown rice, arame, coriander (cilantro), mushrooms with the liquidized tofu mixture.

6. Oil a ring mould and arrange the peppers inside.

7. Add the rice mixture and bake at 325°F/170°C (Gas Mark 3) for approximately 45 minutes until brown on the top.

8. To turn out, run the tin under cold water until the rice is released from the dish, or leave to cool in the tin.

9. Serve hot with steamed broccoli and chunks of tofu or cold with watercress and iced tofu in the middle.

Variation:
Substitute 6 oz (150g/1 cupful) mashed cooked beans for the pine
and cashew nuts.

CHAPATI LAYER

Chapati:

Imperial (Metric)	**American**
½ lb (200g) wholemeal flour	2 cupsful wholewheat flour
Juice of ½ lemon	Juice of ½ lemon
Boiling water	Boiling water

1. Mix the lemon juice, flour and boiling water to make a soft dough. Leave the dough to cool for a while.

2. When cool, break it into small balls (1¼-inches/3cm) and knead the individual balls of dough until smooth but still soft. (Like most wholefood baking, the softer the dough the lighter the food.)

3. When rolling out the chapatis it is important never to put flour onto the rolling out surface. Keep dipping the chapati into a dish of flour. If you do not do this, the surplus flour will burn when cooking the chapati.

4. When rolled out, cook the chapati immediately.

5. Lay out a clean cloth ready for the cooked chapatis.

6. Heat a flat frying pan or 'tarva'.

7. Cook the chapatis so they are dry on both sides; they should bubble a little.

8. Stack one on top of the other wrapped in the cloth. Serve with Bean Sauce.

Bean Sauce:

Imperial (Metric)	American
6 oz (150g) raw kidney beans	1 cupful raw kidney beans
1 clove garlic	1 clove garlic
2 onions	2 onions
1 pint (570ml) Tomato Sauce (page 31)	2½ cupsful Tomato Sauce (page 31)
1 small chilli	1 small chili
1 oz (25g) fresh mint *or* fresh coriander	1 ounce fresh mint *or* cilantro
1 tablespoonful cold-pressed corn oil	1 tablespoonful cold-pressed corn oil
1 teaspoonful fenugreek seeds	1 teaspoonful fenugreek seeds
2 oz (50g) fresh ginger	2 ounces fresh ginger
1 teaspoonful turmeric	1 teaspoonful turmeric

1. Soak the beans with the garlic clove in water (this enhances their flavour).

2. Chop the onions roughly. Liquidize the onions in the tomato sauce.

3. Chop the chilli very finely taking care not to put your fingers near your eyes as the acid given off the chilli can really burn.

4. Grate the ginger.

5. Chop the mint or coriander (cilantro) very finely.

6. Cook the beans — test for softness by pressing between the middle finger and thumb.

7. Heat the oil and add the fenugreek seeds until they pop.

8. Add the chilli and ginger.

9. Add the Tomato Sauce with onions and the cooked beans.

10. Simmer the mixture until the beans become really soft and add the turmeric.

11. Serve hot between chapatis and sprinkle mint or coriander (cilantro) on the top.

SPAGHETTI AND NUT BALLS

Imperial (Metric)	American
½ lb (200g) onions	8 ounces onions
4 cloves garlic	4 cloves garlic
4 oz (100g) sesame seeds	¾ cupful sesame seeds
4 oz (100g) peanuts	¾ cupful peanuts
4 oz (100g) cashew nuts	¾ cupful cashew nuts
2 oz (50g) gram flour	½ cupful gram flour
1 teaspoonful fresh *or* ½ teaspoonful dried oregano	1 teaspoonful fresh *or* ½ teaspoonful dried oregano
1 lb (400g) buckwheat spaghetti	1 pound buckwheat spaghetti
Tomato Sauce (page 31)	Tomato Sauce (page 31)

1. Peel and chop onion into quarters. Peel the garlic.

2. Grind all the nuts and sesame seeds very finely.

3. Liquidize the onions and garlic with 3 tablespoonsful water.

4. Mix the ground nuts, liquidized onion and garlic, gram flour and add the oregano.

5. Shape the nut mixture into small (1¼-inch/3cm) balls. If the mixture sticks use water to dip your hands in — do not use flour.

6. Place the balls in the fridge for at least 1 hour. (I find this a good tip for getting any nut rissole, bean burger, etc., to stick together when cooking.)

7. Cook the spaghetti in boiling water with a little oil. The oil stops the spaghetti sticking together.

8. Deep-fry, shallow-fry or bake the nut balls and serve with Tomato Sauce (page 31).

Note: You can serve this dish with Parmesan cheese which has a sodium content of 760mg per 4 ounces (100g). The average serving of Parmesan is usually 1 ounce (25g) therefore being equal to 190mg per person. Or you can use finely grated horseradish, which is considerably lower in sodium e.g. 8mg per 4 ounces (100g). But, if you choose horseradish, use it sparingly.

TOFU LASAGNE

Imperial (Metric)	American
4 oz (100g) mushrooms	2 cupsful mushrooms
4 oz (100g) celery	4 ounces celery
2 oz (50g) fennel	2 ounces fennel
4 oz (100g) tomatoes	4 ounces tomatoes
½ lb (200g) onions	8 ounces onions
4 oz (100g) spinach	4 ounces spinach
1 oz (25g) fresh herbs	1 ounce fresh herbs
1 oz (25g) tamarind	1 ounce tamarind
½ lb (200g) wholemeal lasagne	8 ounces wholewheat lasagne
4 oz (100g) cooked beans (any type)	⅔ cupful cooked beans (any type)
1 lb (400g) tofu	1 pound tofu
1 teaspoonful cumin and coriander, mixed	1 teaspoonful cumin and coriander, mixed
1 tablespoonful mustard seeds	1 tablespoonful mustard seeds
1 tablespoonful gomasio (optional)	1 tablespoonful gomasio (optional)

1. Clean and chop all the vegetables very finely. The finer the vegetables, the nicer the flavour. Clean and finely chop the herbs. Soak the tamarind in ½ pint (285ml/1⅓ cupsful) water.

2. Place a pan of water on the stove and, when boiling, drop in the lasagne and cook for 4 minutes. (It does not need to be too soft as it will bake for a considerable time when made into the dish.)

3. Mix the herbs, beans and finely chopped vegetables together.

4. In a liquidizer mix together tofu, cumin and coriander, mustard seed and gomasio. Add the soaking water and tamarind and liquidize until of a thin sauce consistency.

5. Lightly oil a deep dish and layer the lasagne and vegetables.

6. Cover the lasagne and vegetables with the tofu sauce. Ease the sauce under the lasagne with a fork.

7. Bake at 250°F/130°C (Gas Mark ½) for 1¼ hours. Serve with a Waldorf salad and grilled fresh tomatoes.

BEAN CASSEROLE

Imperial (Metric)	American
6 oz (150g) dried black beans	1 cupful dried black beans
½ lb (200g) whole shallots or ½ lb (200g) small, firm mushrooms	8 ounces whole shallots or 4 cupsful small, firm mushrooms
½ lb (200g) red peppers	8 ounces red peppers
1 oz (25g) arame (sea vegetable)	1 ounce arame (sea vegetable)
3 tablespoonsful cold-pressed safflower oil	3 tablespoonsful cold-pressed safflower oil
1 teaspoonful nutmeg	1 teaspoonful nutmeg
½ teaspoonful cloves	½ teaspoonful cloves
½ teaspoonful cinnamon	½ teaspoonful cinnamon
2 bay leaves	2 bay leaves
½ lb (200g) yogurt or silken tofu	1 cupful yogurt or silken tofu
4 oz (100g) fresh coriander (chopped for garnish)	4 ounces cilantro (chopped for garnish)

1. Soak the beans (make sure they are thoroughly soaked by breaking open a bean and checking that there are no white patches).

2. Peel the shallots, if using, or wipe the mushrooms.

3. Wash and slice the red peppers.

4. Place the arame in 1 pint (570ml) water.

5. Sauté the peppers, shallots (if used) and arame in safflower oil. Add the soaked beans, nutmeg, cloves and cinnamon. Add the soaking water, bay leaves and mushrooms (if used).

6. Place in a casserole and bake at 250°F/130°C (Gas Mark ½) for 2¼ hours.

7. Serve with yogurt mixed into the liquid just before serving.

8. Take care that the casserole does not boil dry when baking, but do not add too much water as this detracts from the flavour.

VEGETABLE TRIANGLES

Imperial (Metric)	**American**
1 lb (400g) potatoes	1 pound potatoes
4 oz (100g) green beans	2/3 cupful green beans
2 oz (50g) wholemeal flour	1/2 cupful wholewheat flour
1 tablespoonful black mustard seeds	1 tablespoonful black mustard seeds
1 tablespoonful cumin seeds	1 tablespoonful cumin seeds
2 tablespoonsful oil or 1/4 pint (140ml) water	2 tablespoonsful oil or 2/3 cupful water
4 oz (100g) sweetcorn	2/3 cupful sweetcorn
4 oz (100g) peas	2/3 cupful peas
8 very thin chapati (page 50)	8 very thin chapati (page 50)
Juice of 1 lemon	Juice of 1 lemon
1 teaspoonful malt	1 teaspoonful malt

1. Scrub and dice the potatoes into ½-inch (1cm) cubes. Scrub and dice the green beans.

2. Mix together the flour with enough water to make a thick paste.

3. Sauté the mustard and cumin seeds in oil or water.

4. Add the potato, sweetcorn, beans and peas and leave to steam in a pan with a tightly fitting lid.

5. Cut the chapati into quarters.

6. Make a paste of flour and water — water alone will not stick the chapati together. Brush the paste around the sides.

7. Place the filling in the middle and fold the sides over to make a fan shape.

8. Press the sides down well with a fork or spoon handle.

9. Place the envelopes on a baking sheet or grill pan, brush very sparingly with oil and cook until golden-brown — 15 minutes in a grill and 25 minutes in the oven at 300°F/150°C (Gas Mark 2). Serve with banana chutney and green salad.

FENUGREEK PANCAKES

Imperial (Metric)	**American**
1 bunch fresh fenugreek	1 bunch fresh fenugreek (8 ounces)
(½ lb/200g)	1 small chili
1 small chilli	⅔ cupful wholewheat flour
2 oz (50g) wholemeal flour	⅔ cupful rice flour
2 oz (50g) rice flour	1¼ cupsful gram flour
4 oz (100g) gram flour	1 tablespoonful turmeric
1 tablespoonful turmeric	½ cupful plain yogurt
4 fl oz (120ml) natural yogurt	1 tablespoonful homemade Baking
1 tablespoonful homemade Baking	Powder (page 14)
Powder (page 14)	Oil for cooking
Oil for cooking	

1. Wash and chop the fenugreek. Chop the chilli very finely.

2. Mix the flours together. Add the turmeric, fenugreek, chilli, yogurt to the flours. Mix all together with water to a thin batter and leave to stand overnight.

3. Just before cooking, add the Baking Powder to the pancake batter. Lightly oil the pan.

4. Beat the batter well and place 1 spoonful in the pan. Place 1 tablespoonful of oil on top of the pancake and turn to cook. This is a slightly unusual method, but if you oil the pan before the batter is placed in it it tends to burn, so by putting the oil on top of the pancakes they are less likely to stick and this saves oiling the pan every time.

5. Cook the pancakes in a small pan and serve piled three high with Tomato Sauce (page 31).

CAULIFLOWER IN SAUCE

Imperial (Metric)	**American**
1 medium cauliflower	1 medium cauliflower
3 bay leaves	3 bay leaves
1½ oz (36g) sesame seeds	¼ cupful sesame seeds
2 tablespoonsful cold-pressed sesame seed oil	2 tablespoonsful cold-pressed sesame seed oil
1 oz (25g) wholemeal flour	¼ cupful wholewheat flour
½ pint (250ml) vegetable stock, juice from Creamy Mushrooms (page 70), *or* seaweed water	1⅓ cupsful vegetable stock, juice from Creamy Mushrooms (page 70) *or* seaweed water
½ teaspoonful pepper	½ teaspoonful pepper
6 blades mace	6 blades mace
Bouquet garni	*Bouquet garni*

1. Wash the cauliflower and steam with the bay leaves.

2. Roast the sesame seeds.

3. Heat oil and add flour.

4. Gently add stock, stirring constantly so the sauce does not go lumpy.

5. When all the stock has been added, add the pepper, mace and *bouquet garni*.

6. Gently simmer for 20 minutes until the sauce thickens.

7. Pour the sauce over the cauliflower and sprinkle with roasted sesame seeds.

VEGETABLE CANNELLONI

Imperial (Metric)	American
2 oz (50g) peanuts	3½ tablespoonsful peanuts
2 oz (50g) sunflower seeds	½ cupful sunflower seeds
4 oz (100g) fennel	4 ounces fennel
4 oz (100g) mushrooms	2 cupsful mushrooms
4 oz (100g) celery	4 ounces celery
4 oz (100g) red peppers	4 ounces red peppers
2 oz (50g) spring onions	2 ounces scallions
1 tablespoonful fresh oregano	1 tablespoonful fresh oregano
1 teaspoonful fresh basil	1 teaspoonful fresh basil
1 teaspoonful soya oil	1 teaspoonful soy oil
1 lb (400g) wholemeal cannelloni	1 pound wholewheat cannelloni
3 cloves garlic, chopped	3 cloves garlic, chopped
1 tablespoonful cold-pressed safflower oil	1 tablespoonful cold-pressed safflower oil
4 oz (100g) cooked butter beans	⅔ cupful cooked lima beans
½ lb (200g) yogurt or silken tofu	1 cupful yogurt or silken tofu
1 teaspoonful lemon juice	1 teaspoonful lemon juice
½ teaspoonful ground sesame seeds	½ teaspoonful ground sesame seeds
½ teaspoonful aniseed	½ teaspoonful aniseed
½ lb (200g) grated cheese	2 cupsful grated cheese
2 tomatoes	2 tomatoes

1. Grind the peanuts and sunflower seeds together.

2. Finely chop the fennel, mushrooms, celery, peppers, spring onions (scallions), oregano and basil. (The finer the vegetables the nicer the flavour.)

3. Place a pan of water on the heat and bring to the boil.

4. Add the soya oil to the water — this prevents the cannelloni sticking together. Cook the cannelloni until *al dente*.

5. Sauté the spring onions (scallions), basil, garlic and oregano in the safflower oil and add all the finely chopped vegetables.

6. Mash the beans and add, with the ground nuts, to the vegetable mixture.

7. Fill the cannelloni cases with the mixture and lay in a lightly oiled dish.

8. Make the sauce by liquidizing all of the ingredients together adding more water to get a smooth pouring sauce. Cover the cannelloni with the sauce.

9. Garnish with sliced tomato and bake at 300°F/150°C (Gas Mark 2) for 1¼ hours.

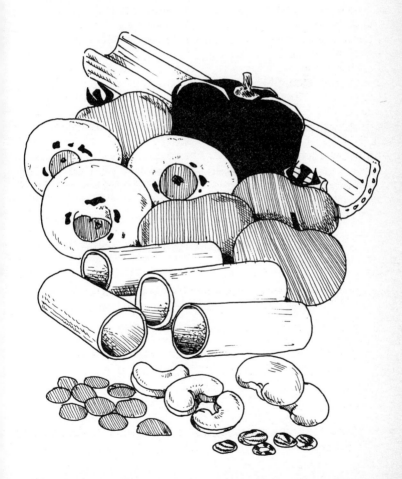

PARSNIP PATTIES

Imperial (Metric)	American
1 lb (400g) parsnips	1 pound parsnips
3 oz (75g) sunflower seeds	1/2 cupful sunflower seeds
4 oz (100g) fresh spinach	4 ounces fresh spinach
2 oz (50g) soya flour	1/2 cupful soy flour
1 tablespoonful turmeric	1 tablespoonful turmeric
6 oz (150g) wholemeal breadcrumbs	3 cupsful wholewheat breadcrumbs
2 oz (50g) fresh sage, chopped	2 ounces fresh sage, chopped
4 oz (100g) sesame seeds	3/4 cupful sesame seeds

1. Steam the parsnips, and mash.

2. Grind the sunflower seeds.

3. Steam the spinach and chop finely.

4. Dissolve the soya flour in a little water.

5. Mix together the turmeric, parsnips, breadcrumbs, spinach, ground sunflower seeds and chopped sage.

6. Add the dissolved soya flour and mix well with parsnip mixture.

7. Shape the parsnip mixture into patties and toss in sesame seeds.

8. Place on an oiled baking sheet and bake at 350°F/180°C (Gas Mark 4) for 40 minutes or shallow fry. Serve with chutney.

TANGY PASTA SHELLS

Imperial (Metric)	**American**
1 clove garlic	1 clove garlic
1 tablespoonful tahini (light)	1 tablespoonful tahini (light)
4 tablespoonsful yogurt cheese	4 tablespoonsful yogurt cheese
3 tablespoonsful Tomato Sauce (page 31)	3 tablespoonsful Tomato Sauce (page 31)
1 teaspoonful fresh lemon juice	1 teaspoonful fresh lemon juice
½ lb (200g) cooked wholemeal pasta shells	8 ounces cooked wholewheat pasta shells

1. Squeeze the garlic into the tahini, add the Yogurt Cheese and Tomato Sauce and mix well together.

2. Mix the lemon juice into the tahini mixture — this will then stiffen.

3. Place the mixture into a piping bag and pipe into the shells.

4. Serve on a bed of sliced red peppers.

MILLET AND CHICK PEA STEW

Imperial (Metric)	American
2 oz (50g) chick peas	¼ cupful garbanzo beans
1 bunch spring onions	1 bunch scallions
2 cloves garlic	2 cloves garlic
3 sticks celery *or* fennel	3 stalks celery *or* 3 pieces fennel
2 carrots	2 carrots
½-inch (1cm) cube fresh ginger	½-inch cube fresh ginger
1 teaspoonful Sprinkle (page 22)	1 teaspoonful Sprinkle (page 22)
2 tablespoonsful cold-pressed sesame oil	2 tablespoonsful cold-pressed sesame oil
4 oz (100g) millet	½ cupful millet
1 piece wakame (sea vegetable)	1 piece wakame (sea vegetable)
4 oz (100g) mushrooms	2 cupsful mushrooms
Fresh coriander for garnish	Cilantro for garnish

1. Soak and cook the chick peas (garbanzos) for 20 minutes in a pressure cooker or 1¼ hours in a saucepan with a tightly fitting lid. Reserve the water.

2. Wash and chop the spring onions (scallions), garlic, celery or fennel and dice the carrots. Grate the ginger.

3. Sauté the garlic, Sprinkle, ginger and celery or fennel in the sesame oil until brown.

4. Add the carrots, chick peas (garbanzos), onions, millet, reserved water and wakame.

5. Simmer for 25-35 minutes until the millet is soft. Do not stir the stew until the millet is soft.

6. Add the whole mushrooms, remove from the heat, leave for 5 minutes with the lid on and then serve, garnished with coriander (cilantro).

SUNBURGERS
Makes 6

Imperial (Metric)	American
½ lb (200g) sunflower seeds	1½ cupful sunflower seeds
1 large onion	1 large onion
1 egg, beaten, *or* 2 tablespoonsful tahini	1 egg, beaten, *or* 2 tablespoonsful tahini
1 green pepper	1 green pepper
1 tablespoonful fresh thyme	1 tablespoonful fresh thyme
4 oz (100g) grated carrot	⅔ cupful grated carrot
4 oz (100g) wholemeal breadcrumbs	2 cupsful wholewheat breadcrumbs
1 teaspoonful dal masala *or* curry powder	1 teaspoonful dal masala *or* curry powder
Sesame seeds for coating	Sesame seeds for coating

1. Roast the sunflower seeds and grind them finely.

2. Liquidize the onion in the egg or tahini.

3. Wash and chop the green pepper very finely.

4. Wash and chop the thyme.

5. Mix together the ground sunflower seeds, liquidized onion, finely chopped pepper, grated carrot, thyme, breadcrumbs, dal masala and shape into burgers.

6. Brush with water and coat in sesame seeds.

7. Bake at any temperature until a golden brown — serve with Tomato Sauce (page 31) and Apple Crunch Sauce (page 35).

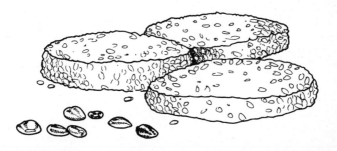

BEAN BURGERS
Makes 10

Imperial (Metric)	American
4 oz (100g) green lentils	½ cupful green lentils
2 medium potatoes	2 medium potatoes
(approx 10 oz/250g)	(approx 10 ounces)
3 oz (75g) wholemeal breadcrumbs	1½ cupsful wholewheat
4 oz (100g) peanuts	breadcrumbs
1 oz (25g) sesame seeds	¾ cupful peanuts
1 onion	3 tablespoonsful sesame seeds
1 tablespoonful chopped parsley	1 onion
1 egg, beaten	1 tablespoonful chopped parsley
1 tablespoonful ground coriander	1 egg, beaten
	1 tablespoonful ground cilantro

1. Soak the lentils for 2 hours, wash well and remove any stones. Cook until soft and drain well.

2. Boil the potatoes in their skins, peel and mash.

3. Grind the breadcrumbs, peanuts and sesame seeds.

4. Peel and chop the onion very finely. Wash and chop the parsley.

5. Combine all the ingredients together and shape into burgers. If the mixture sticks, dip your hands into cold water — do not use flour, this makes it worse.

6. Place on a lightly-oiled tin and bake or shallow fry, barbecue or grill until golden-brown.

3.

VEGETABLE DISHES
AND SALADS

STIR-FRY

Imperial (Metric)	American
1 bunch spring onions	1 bunch scallions
6 sticks celery	6 stalks celery
½ teaspoonful cold-pressed sesame seed oil *or* ghee	½ teaspoonful cold-pressed sesame seed oil *or* ghee
1 teaspoonful mustard seeds	1 teaspoonful mustard seeds
½ lb (200g) fenugreek sprouts	8 ounces fenugreek sprouts

1. Wash and slice the spring onions (scallions) into rings. Chop the celery very finely.

2. Heat the oil or melt the ghee slowly in a wok. When the fat is hot add the mustard seeds. Have a lid ready for the wok as the seeds will pop.

3. When the seeds have popped, turn off the heat and add the fenugreek sprouts, spring onions (scallions) and chopped celery. The vegetables should cook very quickly — keep turning and stirring. Take care not to overcook the vegetables, they should be crisp and tasty. Serve immediately.

How to Sprout Fenugreek:

Imperial (Metric)   **American**
1 oz (25g) fenugreek seeds   3 tablespoonsful fenugreek seeds

1. Leave the seeds to soak in water overnight.

2. Drain the water off and place the seeds in a jar. Cover the jar
    with muslin or a piece of fine net curtaining. Take care when
    choosing the jar that there is lots of room, as the seeds increase
    by about 10 times in volume. Make sure the jar is kept out of
    direct sunlight — you can use a brown jar or cover it with a paper
    bag to achieve this.

3. Water the seeds. Do not run the seeds under cold water, use water
    of room temperature. Rinse the sprouts twice a day, after rinsing
    leave the jar propped up on the draining board, so excess water
    can drain away. Do not shake the sprouts as they are liable to break.

4. Fenugreek sprouts are ready to use in 3-4 days. They have a
    slightly bitter curry flavour. To avoid a bitter flavour they must
    be well rinsed when growing.

Note: The same method can be used for alfalfa, moong beans,
sunflower seeds, beans and peas. Do not sprout kidney or soya beans
as they must be boiled for at least 10 minutes to destroy toxins in
the beans.

WHITE STIR-FRY

Imperial (Metric)	American
6 oz (150g) white radish	6 ounces white radish
½ lb (200g) turnips	8 ounces turnips
10 oz (250g) parsnips	10 ounces parsnips
½ lb (200g) leeks	8 ounces leeks
2 inches (5cm) horseradish root	2 inches horseradish root
10 oz (250g) apples	10 ounces apples
1 tablespoonful lemon juice	1 tablespoonful lemon juice
1 teaspoonful corn oil *or* ghee	1 teaspoonful corn oil *or* ghee
1 tablespoonful sesame seeds	1 tablespoonful sesame seeds
½ teaspoonful garam masala	½ teaspoonful garam masala (curry powder)
1 tablespoonful concentrated apple juice	1 tablespoonful concentrated apple juice

1. Wash and slice the radish, turnip, parsnip and leeks. Cut the slices into half or quarter circles of approximately the same size. Grate the horseradish on a very fine grater.

2. Clean and grate the apples, do not remove skin, and sprinkle with lemon juice.

3. In a wok heat the oil or ghee. When hot add the sesame seeds, garam masala and grated horseradish.

4. Turn off heat and add parsnips, leeks, turnip and white radish.

5. Turn heat back on and stir the vegetables, so they are covered in oil. Place lid on the wok, turn heat down low and leave to steam.

6. Serve with grated apple and apple juice on top.

VEGETABLE KEBABS

For the marinade:

Imperial (Metric)	American
1 teaspoonful garam masala	1 teaspoonful garam masala
1 tablespoonful cumin powder	1 tablespoonful cumin powder
3 tablespoonsful cold-pressed sesame oil	3 tablespoonsful cold-pressed sesame oil
Juice of ½ lemon	Juice of ½ lemon
¼ teaspoonful black pepper	¼ teaspoonful black pepper
¼ teaspoonful fresh *or* a pinch of dried rosemary	¼ teaspoonful fresh *or* a pinch of dried rosemary

1. Mix all the marinade ingredients together in a jam jar with a screw top lid and shake well.

For the kebabs:

Mushrooms — firm, whole
Green or red pepper — square pieces
Onions — small, whole *or* spring onions (scallions)
Tomatoes — small whole tomatoes
Aubergine (Eggplant) — cubes approximately 1¼-inches (2.5cm) square
Banana — very firm but ripe chunks
Tofu — 1-inch (2cm) squares
Tempeh — 1-inch (2cm) squares
Spinach — rolled up into rolls approximately 1-inch (2cm) thick
Beetroot (beet) — small, whole
Cauliflower — florettes
Apple — square chunks

1. Place whichever pieces of fruit and vegetables you choose on a skewer, making sure when you prepare the food that the size of each item is appropriate to its cooking time. That is, things which cook slowly must be cut smaller, so that everything is ready at the same moment.

2. Brush on the marinade and either grill or bake on a barbecue. Serve hot on a bed of rice with Coconut Chutney

POTATOES AND CORN

Imperial (Metric)	American
1 lb (400g) potatoes	1 pound potatoes
4 oz (100g) corn kernels	⅔ cupful corn kernels
½ teaspoonful sesame seed oil *or* ghee	½ teaspoonful sesame seed oil *or* ghee
1 teaspoonful mustard seeds	1 teaspoonful mustard seeds
2 cloves garlic, finely chopped	2 cloves garlic, finely chopped
½ teaspoonful cumin powder	½ teaspoonful cumin powder
1 teaspoonful coriander seeds	1 teaspoonful cilantro seeds
2 oz (50g) freshly chopped chives, for garnish	2 ounces freshly chopped chives, for garnish

1. Clean and cook the potatoes by steaming, boiling or baking. Steam the corn.

2. Place the oil or ghee in a saucepan and add mustard seed and garlic. Heat gently, covered with a lid, till the mustard seeds pop. Add the cumin and coriander.

3. Place the cooked potatoes and corn in the saucepan and mix well. Leave the dish to marinate for 2-3 hours and serve cold as a salad or re-heat as a vegetable dish. Garnish with chopped chives.

CREAMY MUSHROOMS

Imperial (Metric)
2 cloves garlic, finely chopped
1 oz (25g) tamarind flowers, finely
  chopped
1 tablespoonful cold-pressed
  sunflower oil *or* ghee
4 oz (100g) small mushrooms,
  cleaned
1 teaspoonful freshly ground black
  pepper
4 fl oz (120ml) yogurt

American
2 cloves garlic, finely chopped
1 ounce tamarind flowers, finely
  chopped
1 tablespoonful cold-pressed
  sunflower oil *or* ghee
2 cupsful small mushrooms, cleaned
1 teaspoonful freshly ground black
  pepper
½ cupful yogurt

1. Sauté the garlic and tamarind in oil or ghee.

2. Add the mushrooms and toss in the sautéed ingredients until all of the oil is absorbed. Season with pepper.

3. Add the yogurt and serve hot or cold. (As the mixture cools a liquid is given off — strain this off but do not throw it away as it is very tasty and can be used in cooking.)

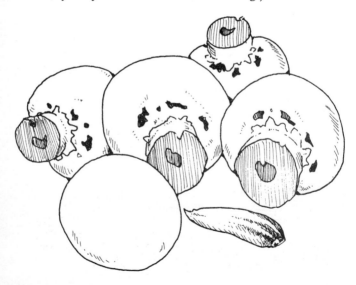

BLACK BEAN MARINADE

Imperial (Metric)	American
4 oz (100g) black beans, soaked overnight	²⁄₃ cupful black beans, soaked overnight
1 tablespoonful wine *or* rice vinegar	1 tablespoonful wine *or* rice vinegar
1 clove garlic, peeled	1 clove garlic, peeled
1 teaspoonful cloves	1 teaspoonful cloves
½ teaspoonful nutmeg	½ teaspoonful nutmeg
½ teaspoonful chilli	½ teasponful chili
1 tablespoonful olive oil *or* lemon juice	1 tablespoonful olive oil *or* lemon juice

1. Cook the beans until soft when squeezed between the thumb and middle finger, 30 minutes in a pressure cooker, 1¼ hours in a saucepan on the stove.

2. Liquidize the vinegar, garlic, cloves, nutmeg, chilli and olive oil or lemon juice.

3. Skewer the beans on cocktail sticks and place in the marinade. Leave them for a while and then serve on rice or with Potato Salad (page 76).

Note: Beans that have been in a marinade can be used in salad and this often means that the salads do not have to be dressed.

RICE AND JUNIPER BERRIES

Imperial (Metric)
½ lb (200g) brown rice
2 oz (50g) juniper berries, lightly
  crushed

American
1 cupful brown rice
½ cupful juniper berries, lightly
  crushed

1. Wash the brown rice very well.

2. Choose a saucepan with a tightly fitting lid and put the rice in it.

3. Add twice the volume of water to rice, add the juniper berries and bring to the boil. Do *not* stir at any point during cooking.

4. When the rice starts to boil, turn the heat down to a simmer, keeping the lid on the saucepan.

5. After approximately 25 minutes the water will have boiled away. Leave the pan on the stove, turn off the heat and allow to steam for a further 20 minutes with the lid on.

Note: To pressure cook this dish, put the washed rice and 1½ times its volume in water into a pressure cooker with the juniper berries and cook for about 20 minutes.

WHOLE GREEN BEANS

Imperial (Metric)
½-inch (1cm) cube root ginger
1 teaspoonful fenugreek powder
2 tablespoonsful finely chopped
    fresh mint
1 lb (400g) whole green French
    beans
1 teaspoonful olive oil (optional)

American
½-inch cube root ginger
1 teaspoonful fenugreek powder
2 tablespoonsful finely chopped
    fresh mint
1 pound whole green snap beans
1 teaspoonful olive oil (optional)

1. Wash and clean the beans. Grate the ginger finely.

2. In a saucepan place enough water to cover the bottom and heat.
    Add the fenugreek powder and grated ginger.

3. Add the beans and mint and toss in the mixture. Continue to
    cook them until they are soft and brilliant green in colour. They
    can be served hot, straight from the pan, or cold with the ginger
    mixture as a marinade. Whether served hot or cold, they can be
    tossed in olive oil.

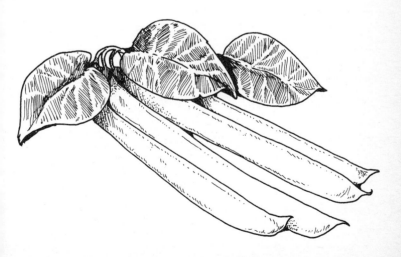

TEMPURA

Imperial (Metric)	American
Finely sliced vegetables — e.g. cabbage and onion, potatoes and onion, cauliflower and broccoli	Finely sliced vegetables — e.g. cabbage and onion, potatoes and onion, cauliflower and broccoli
½ lb (200g) gram flour	1½ cupsful gram flour
1 tablespoonful coriander	1 tablespoonful cilantro
1 teaspoonful ground mustard seeds	1 teaspoonful ground mustard seeds
1 teaspoonful celery seeds	1 teaspoonful celery seeds
2 tablespoonsful chopped fresh oregano	2 tablespoonsful chopped fresh oregano
Safflower oil for frying	Safflower oil for frying

1. Slice the vegetables *very* finely — this is most important otherwise they will not cook thoroughly. Mushrooms are an exception and can be cooked whole.

2. Mix all of the dry ingredients together and add enough water to form a coating batter, i.e., it should coat the back of the spoon.

3. Dry the vegetables well with kitchen paper or cloth, paying special attention to courgette (zucchini) or marrow (squash) if used. Mix the vegetables into the batter.

4. Heat the oil and test for use by putting a little of the batter into the hot fat. If it rises immediately it is ready, if it sinks wait a few minutes more as it is most important that the fat is hot enough.

5. Place tablespoonsful of the battered vegetables *(tempura)* in the oil and cook until golden brown, drain well and serve hot, or cold in lunch boxes.

MELON, TOMATO AND CUCUMBER SALAD

Imperial (Metric)	American
1 cantaloupe melon	1 cantaloupe melon
1 cucumber	1 cucumber
1 lb (400g) tomatoes	1 pound tomatoes
2 oz (50g) lemon balm leaves	2 ounces lemon balm leaves

1. Slice and cube the melon.

2. Cut the cucumber into cubes.

3. Slice the tomatoes into 'moon' shapes.

4. Chop the lemon balm leaves very finely.

5. Mix all the ingredients, except the lemon balm, together and serve chilled, garnished with the lemon balm.

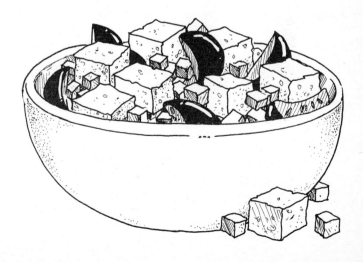

POTATO SALAD

Imperial (Metric)
1 lb (400g) diced cooked potato
½ lb (200g) celery
2 oz (50g) fresh mint
2 oz (50g) fresh coriander
3 oz (75g) natural yogurt *or* silken tofu
Pinch chilli powder
Pinch turmeric
Crisp lettuce leaves
Celery leaves, mint leaves and rose petals for garnish

American
2⅔ cupsful diced cooked potato
8 ounces celery
2 ounces fresh mint
2 ounces cilantro
⅓ cupful plain yogurt *or* silken tofu
Pinch chili powder
Pinch turmeric
Crisp lettuce leaves
Celery leaves, mint leaves and rose petals for garnish

1. Scrub and chop celery very finely.

2. Wash and chop the fresh mint — apple or lemon mint is best for this dish and dried mint is awful!

3. Wash and chop the coriander (cilantro) very finely.

4. Mix all of the ingredients together and serve on a bed of crisp lettuce garnished with the celery leaves, mint leaves and rose petals.

TOMATO SALAD

Imperial (Metric)	American
1 tablespoonful fresh *or* ½ tablespoonful dried tarragon	1 tablespoonful fresh *or* ½ tablespoonful dried tarragon
1 lb (400g) tomatoes	1 pound tomatoes

Dressing:

Imperial (Metric)	American
1 tablespoonful freshly chopped mint	1 tablespoonful freshly chopped mint
1 teaspoonful apple juice	1 teaspoonful apple juice
1 teaspoonful cider vinegar	1 teaspoonful cider vinegar
1 tablespoonful cold-pressed sesame oil	1 tablespoonful cold-pressed sesame oil

1. Wash and finely chop the tarragon, if using fresh.

2. On the same chopping board, slice the tomatoes into rings.

3. Mix the tomatoes and tarragon together.

4. Place all the dressing ingredients in a jar with a lid and shake well.

5. Dress the tomatoes and chill before serving. A refreshing salad suitable for serving with any grain dish.

RED KIDNEY BEAN AND CABBAGE SALAD

Imperial (Metric)	American
4 oz (100g) red kidney beans	½ cupful red kidney beans
½ lb (200g) cabbage	8 ounces cabbage
1 large apple	1 large apple
½ oz (12g) fresh tarragon	½ ounce fresh tarragon
1 tablespoonful white wine vinegar	1 tablespoonful white wine vinegar
1 teaspoonful olive oil	1 teaspoonful olive oil

1. Soak the red kidney beans overnight. Cook the kidney beans until you can squeeze them between the thumb and middle finger. Do not overcook them for salads as they can taste soggy when mixed with the vegetables. Leave to cool.

2. Shred the cabbage finely. Grate the apple. Wash and chop the fresh tarragon very finely.

3. Mix the vinegar, oil and tarragon together in a jam jar with a lid and shake.

4. Mix together the apple, cabbage, cooked red kidney beans and dressing. Serve immediately.

Note: Red kidney beans must be fast-boiled for a minimum of 10 minutes at the start of cooking to destroy toxins.

TABBOULEH

Imperial (Metric)	American
2 cupsful boiling water	2½ cupsful boiling water
½ lb (200g) bulgar	1⅓ cupsful bulgar
1 lemon	1 lemon
2 cloves garlic	2 cloves garlic
3 tablespoonsful olive oil	3 tablespoonsful olive oil
2 oz (50g) fresh mint, chopped very fine	2 ounces fresh mint, chopped very fine
2 oz (50g) fresh parsley, chopped very fine	2 ounces fresh parsley, chopped very fine
½ teaspoonful grated horseradish root	½ teaspoonful grated horseradish root
Freshly ground black pepper	Freshly ground black pepper
1 bunch spring onions, chopped	1 bunch scallions, chopped

1. Pour the boiling water onto the bulgar and leave to stand — do not stir.

2. Grate the rind of the lemon finely and squeeze the juice. Mix together.

3. Peel and chop or crush the garlic and mix it into the lemon juice.

4. Mix together the lemon and garlic mixture with the olive oil, mint, parsley, horseradish and black pepper.

5. When the bulgar has absorbed all of the water, mix together with the herb/lemon mixture.

6. Sprinkle the chopped spring onions (scallions) on the top of the Tabbouleh.

STEAMED CARROTS AND SPROUTS

When using carrots for sodium free cooking, take care always to use young carrots as the sodium content is much lower.

Steaming carrots is a lovely way of preserving the colour of the vegetables but, depending on where the vegetables are grown and how old they are, they can be a little tasteless. By steaming bay leaves with the vegetables the smell of cooking is considerably reduced and the flavour of the vegetables enhanced.

At the time of preparing the carrots think of their final appearance upon serving. Cutting small wedges lengthwise out of the side of the carrots will give the appearance of flowers when the carrots are sliced. Slicing carrots lengthwise with a potato peeler enables them to be rolled when cooked. Diagonally slicing the carrot and cutting it into sticks gives a shape that is pleasing and easy to handle by small children.

For a carrot and Brussels sprouts mixture, use double the quantity of sprouts to carrots. Choose small, tightly-closed young Brussels sprouts.

Clean the vegetables, a vegetable scrubbing brush is enough to clean organic carrots, but if they are not organically grown I would suggest they are thinly peeled.

Place the vegetables in a steamer with 6 bay leaves and place the steamer over boiling water. It takes approximately 20 minutes to steam carrots and sprouts together. You can cook any type of vegetable this way, just make sure if you mix vegetables that they take the same amount of time to cook or they are the same size when being cooked. Remove the bay leaves and leave them to dry so they can be used again.

4.

DESSERTS, CAKES AND BISCUITS

DROP SCONES

Imperial (Metric)	American
½ lb (200g) wholemeal flour	2 cupsful wholewheat flour
2 teaspoonsful Potassium Baking Powder (page 14)	2 teaspoonsful Potassium Baking Powder (page 14)
1 egg *or* 1 heaped tablespoonful soya flour	1 egg *or* 1 heaped tablespoonful soy flour
½ pint (250ml) apple juice	1⅓ cupsful apple juice

1. Place all the dry ingredients in a bowl. Add the egg, if used.

2. Mix to a thick batter with the apple juice. Leave to stand for 20 minutes.

3. Lightly oil a griddle pan or frying pan.

4. Place one tablespoonful of the mixture at a time into the pan or griddle. When bubbles appear on the surface, turn the drop scones over and cook on the other side.

5. Serve hot with sugar-free jam or puréed fruit.

WHOLEWHEAT PANCAKES

Imperial (Metric)
½ lb (200g) wholemeal flour
1 egg *or* 1 heaped tablespoonful
soya flour
1 pint (500ml) apple juice
1 heaped teaspoonful Potassium
Baking Powder (page 14)
Cold-pressed sunflower oil for
cooking

American
2 cupsful wholewheat flour
1 egg *or* 1 heaped tablespoonful soy
flour
2½ cupsful apple juice
1 heaped teaspoonful Potassium
Baking Powder (page 14)
Cold-pressed sunflower oil for
cooking

1. Beat all the ingredients together and leave the mixture to stand. The finer you want the pancakes to be, the longer the batter has to stand. Overnight in the refrigerator gives the best results.

2. Lightly oil a frying pan and heat — do not allow the fat to smoke.

3. Pour a little mixture round the edges of the pan and let it spread to the middle. Cook until the pancake bubbles then turn and cook the other side. Serve with yogurt and puréed fruit.

WAFFLES
Makes 6

Imperial (Metric)	American
½ lb (200g) wholemeal flour	2 cupsful wholewheat flour
2 eggs	2 eggs
1 tablespoonful Potassium Baking Powder (page 14)	1 tablespoonful Potassium Baking Powder (page 14)
1 tablespoonful cold-pressed corn oil	1 tablespoonful cold-pressed corn oil
1 tablespoonful apple juice concentrate	1 tablespoonful apple juice concentrate
Water to mix	Water to mix

1. Mix all the ingredients together, adding the water last, to make a thick batter.

2. Heat a waffle iron. Oil the iron lightly when warm.

3. Pour 1 tablespoonful of the mixture into the waffle iron and spread it over — if you overfill the waffle iron the batter will run out.

4. Turn the iron over and cook the other side.

5. When the waffle is cooked it will drop out of the iron and not have to be forced out with a knife.

6. Serve with maple syrup or sugar-free strawberry jam.

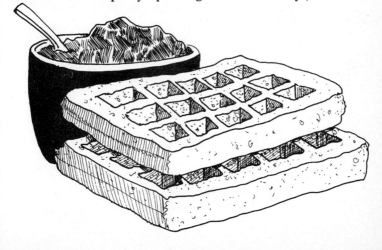

LEMON MERINGUE PIE

Imperial (Metric)	American
3 lemons	3 lemons
3 eggs	3 eggs
1 oz (25g) kudzu *or* arrowroot	2 tablespoonsful kudzu *or* arrowroot
½ pint (250ml) water	1⅓ cupsful water
1 tablespoonful honey	1 tablespoonful honey
1 Salt-free Pastry Case (page 108)	1 Salt-free Pastry Case (page 108)
3 tablespoonsful maple syrup	3 tablespoonsful maple syrup

1. Squeeze the lemons and grate the rind of one lemon finely.

2. Separate the eggs — take care not to get any egg yolk in the white.

3. Dissolve the kudzu or arrowroot in the water and add the honey.

4. Heat the liquid and add the lemon juice and rind.

5. When the liquid thickens, remove from the heat and add the egg yolks. Make sure the yolks are well beaten in. These give the base a rich yellow colour. Pour into the pastry case when cool.

6. Whisk the egg whites until very stiff and add the maple syrup and whisk well.

7. Place the meringue mixture on top of the lemon mix and place in a hot oven 400°F/200°C (Gas Mark 6) for approximately 10 minutes until golden brown.

8. Serve cold. The pie will not be set if served hot.

MILLET PUDDING

Imperial (Metric)
½ lb (200g) mandarin oranges
3 oz (75g) raw millet
2 eggs *or* 2 oz (50g) silken tofu plus
  2 egg whites
3 tablespoonsful apple juice
  concentrate *or* 2 tablespoonsful
  malt

American
½ lb (200g) mandarin oranges
⅓ cupful raw millet
2 eggs *or* ¼ cupful silken tofu plus
  2 egg whites
3 tablespoonsful apple juice
  concentrate *or* 2 tablespoonsful
  malt

1. Peel and chop the mandarin oranges very finely.

2. Place the millet in a saucepan with a tightly fitting lid and heat gently to roast. As soon as the aroma is noticable from the millet, remove from heat. Add double its volume in water, return to the heat and leave to simmer with the lid on. Once the water has been absorbed, remove from the heat, keep the lid firmly on and leave to steam. Never stir the millet while it is cooking. Grains cook from the bottom of the pan and the top grains cook by steaming.

3. Oil an 8-inch (20cm) ovenproof dish lightly.

4. Mix the millet, egg yolks or silken tofu, fruit and apple juice.

5. Whisk the egg whites until very stiff. Add them to the millet mixture and mix well.

6. Place the mixture in the oiled dish and bake at 350°F/180°C (Gas Mark 4) for 20-25 minutes until risen and firm to the touch. Serve with a fruit purée such as apricot or strawberry.

BAKED PARSNIPS WITH MAPLE SYRUP AND CASHEW NUT CREAM

Imperial (Metric)
1 lb (400g) parsnips
4 tablespoonsful maple syrup
2 cardamom pods

American
1 pound parsnips
4 tablespoonsful maple syrup
2 cardamom pods

1. Heat the oven to 350°F/180°C (Gas Mark 4).

2. Scrub the parsnips and cut into quarters lengthways, so they are all of an equal size.

3. Place in an ovenproof dish and cover with water.

4. Add the maple syrup and the black seeds from the cardamom pods.

5. Bake in the pre-heated oven for 40 minutes, when the parsnips should be tender. Serve with Cashew Nut Cream (below).

CASHEW NUT CREAM

Imperial (Metric)
½ lb (200g) cashew nut pieces
1 cardamom pod
½ pint (250ml) water (approx.)

American
1⅔ cupsful cashew nut pieces
1 cardamom pod
1⅓ cupsful water (approx.)

1. Liquidize the nuts, seeds from the cardamom pod and water together. The thickness of the cream is determined by the amount of water used, so you can make it thicker or thiner by using less or more water.

SOYA BEAN BAKE

Imperial (Metric)	American
2 oz (50g) soya beans	⅓ cupful soy beans
¼ teaspoonful dried ginger	¼ teaspoonful dried ginger
½ teaspoonful nutmeg	½ teaspoonful nutmeg
1 teaspoonful cinnamon	1 teaspoonful cinnamon
2 eggs or 4 oz (100g) silken tofu	2 eggs or ½ cupful silken tofu
2 fl oz (60ml) yogurt	¼ cupful yogurt
2 tablespoonsful malt	2 tablespoonsful malt
4 oz (100g) hunza (wild) apricots	¾ cupful hunza (wild) apricots

1. Soak the beans for a minimum of 8 hours or until, when split open, both halves are uniform in colour. There should be no patches on the bean. Cook them until you can press them gently between the thumb and first finger.

2. Liquidize the ginger, nutmeg, cinnamon, eggs, yogurt and malt.

3. Soak the apricots in water or cold tea to cover. When soft, remove the stones and chop into small pieces.

4. Add the soya beans to the eggs, spice and yogurt mixture and liquidize together. Add the chopped apricots and stir well.

5. Pour the mixture into an oiled 6-inch (15cm) ovenproof dish and bake at 400°F/200°C (Gas Mark 6) for approximately 20 minutes until the mixture is set.

Note: Soya beans must be fast-boiled for the first 10 minutes of cooking to destroy toxins within the beans.

Apricots contain only a trace of sodium, but are rich in potassium and have more protein and iron than any other dried fruit. Most apricots are treated with sulphur dioxide so look for shrivelled apricot pieces if you cannot buy hunzas, as the darker the fruit and the more shrivelled the flesh the less likely they are to have been sprayed.

YOGURT

Imperial (Metric)
1½ pints (750ml) milk (you can use
   goat's, cow's or skimmed milk)
6 tablespoonsful natural, live yogurt
2 tablespoonsful powdered milk
   (optional)

American
3¾ cupsful milk (you can use
   goat's, cow's or skimmed milk)
6 tablespoonsful natural, live yogurt
2 tablespoonsful powdered milk
   (optional)

1. Heat the milk to blood temperature in a stainless steel pan (if possible) — test the temperature by putting a cooking thermometer in the pan or by putting a few drops of milk on the back of your hand.

2. Whisk the yogurt into the milk and leave it in a warm place to maintain the temperature for nine hours or overnight.

3. To thicken the yogurt you can either add 2 tablespoonsful of powdered milk or place the yogurt on the top shelf of the refrigerator as near the ice box as possible.

4. The first batch of yogurt is always thin but it thickens with every batch made. Take care when using the yogurt not to leave it uncovered in a warm room before eating as air borne bacteria can enter it, making it taste bitter. Repeat the process to make more yogurt.

'PINK'

Imperial (Metric)
½ lb (200g) cashew nut pieces
4 oz (100g) tofu
½ pint (500ml) red grape juice
1 lb (400g) raspberries

American
1⅔ cupful cashew nut pieces
½ cupful tofu
1⅓ cupful red grape juice
4 cupful raspberries

1. Liquidize the nuts, tofu and grape juice together.

2. Place in glasses with layers of raspberries and serve with raspberries on top and with Vanilla Bites (page 96).

CAROB LOG

Imperial (Metric)
1/2 lb (200g) wholemeal flour
1 level teaspoonful Potassium
  Baking Powder (page 14)
6 tablespoonsful cold-pressed corn
  oil
6 tablespoonsful runny honey
2 tablespoonsful malt
1 egg
2 oz (50g) carob powder

American
2 cupsful wholewheat flour
1 level teaspoonful Potassium
  Baking Powder (page 14)
6 tablespoonsful cold-pressed corn
  oil
6 tablespoonsful runny honey
2 tablespoonsful malt
1 egg
1/2 cupful carob powder

Filling and Topping:

Imperial (Metric)
1/2 lb (200g) yogurt cheese *or* silken
  tofu
1 tablespoonful runny honey
1 tablespoonful *Barleycup*
Sugar-free raspberry jam
4 oz (100g) bar plain carob
  chocolate

American
1 cupful yogurt cheese *or* silken tofu
1 tablespoonful runny honey
1 tablespoonful *Barleycup*
Sugar-free raspberry jam
4 ounce bar plain carob chocolate

1. Lightly oil two baking sheets. Heat the oven to 350°F/180°C (Gas Mark 4).

2. Mix all the ingredients together and spoon in equal amounts onto the baking tin.

3. Bake in the preheated oven for 15-20 minutes. They will be still soft but should be set, and will harden on cooling. When cooled, put together into a log as follows.

4. Mix together the cheese or tofu, honey and *Barleycup*.

5. Sandwich the carob drops together with raspberry jam and stand one behind the other in a log shape.

6. Cover the log with the topping and garnish with grated carob chocolate.

7. Chill for 1 hour and serve.

Variation:
For a more luxurious, cake-type of log, the carob drops can be dipped very quickly in sherry or raspberry liqueur and then sandwiched together with the topping.

MANGO CAKE

Imperial (Metric)	**American**
6 oz (150g) ripe mango	6 ounces ripe mango
2 bananas	2 bananas
4 tablespoonsful cold-pressed corn oil	4 tablespoonsful cold-pressed corn oil
1 dessertspoonful molasses	2 teaspoonsful molasses
2 tablespoonsful malt	2 tablespoonsful malt
2 eggs	2 eggs
4 oz (100g) wholemeal flour	1 cupful wholewheat flour
2 teaspoonsful Potassium Baking Powder (page 14)	2 teaspoonsful Potassium Baking Powder (page 14)

1. Oil and line a Swiss-roll tin. Heat the oven to 350°F/180°C (Gas Mark 4).

2. Peel and cut up the flesh from the mango into small pieces. Peel and cut up the bananas.

3. Beat together the oil, molasses and malt until light and fluffy. (It should be light in colour and well mixed — there should be no oil on the surface.)

4. Beat in the eggs, one at a time. Add the flour, baking powder, bananas and mango.

5. Spread evenly in the lined tin.

6. Place in the pre-heated oven for 20-25 minutes until the cake springs back when lightly pressed.

APPLE AND GRAM CAKES

Imperial (Metric)
½ lb (200g) eating apples
6 oz (150g) gram flour
1 teaspoonful pure vanilla essence
1 tablespoonful Potassium Baking
   Powder (page 14)
1 teaspoonful cinnamon

American
8 ounces eating apples
1 cupful gram flour
1 teaspoonful pure vanilla essence
1 tablespoonful Potassium Baking
   Powder (page 14)
1 teaspoonful cinnamon

1. Wash and grate the apples.

2. Mix together the gram flour, grated apples, vanilla, baking powder and cinnamon. Add enough water to make a thick coating batter.

3. Lightly oil a frying pan (if you have a well-used pan it will not need to be oiled).

4. Place tablespoonsful of the mixture in the heated pan and cook gently, ensuring that the middle also cooks.

5. When bubbles appear on the surface, turn the cakes over and cook until lightly browned. Serve hot with yogurt or maple syrup.

CAROB AND HAZELNUT CAKE

Imperial (Metric)	American
3 tablespoonsful cold-pressed corn oil	3 tablespoonsful cold-pressed corn oil
2 eggs	2 eggs
3 tablespoonsful malt	3 tablespoonsful malt
4 oz (100g) wholemeal flour	1 cupful wholewheat flour
2 oz (50g) carob powder	½ cupful carob powder
1 teaspoonful Potassium Baking Powder (page 14)	1 teaspoonful Potassium Baking Powder (page 14)
2 oz (50g) hazelnut kernels	⅓ cupful hazelnut kernels
1 large orange	1 large orange

1. Heat the oven to 350°F/180°C (Gas Mark 4).

2. Beat the oil, eggs and malt together. Add the flour.

3. Seive the carob flour into the mixture with the baking powder. Add the hazelnuts and stir gently.

4. Oil and prepare an 8-inch (20cm) round cake tin. Place the cake mixture in the tin, spread evenly and bake for 25 minutes in the pre-heated oven.

5. Remove cake from the tin and leave to cool.

6. With a cocktail stick, prick the cake all over the surface and squeeze fresh orange juice over.

7. Serve with Cashew Nut Cream (page 86) or fresh fruit.

SUGAR-FREE FRUIT CAKE

Imperial (Metric)	American
1 cup mixed dried fruit	1¼ cupsful mixed dried fruit
1 teaspoonful mixed spices	1 teaspoonful mixed spices
1 tablespoonful malt extract (optional)	1 tablespoonful malt extract (optional)
4 tablespoonsful cold-pressed corn oil	4 tablespoonsful cold-pressed corn oil
½ lb (200g) wholemeal flour	2 cupsful wholewheat flour
1 teaspoonful Potassium Baking Powder (page 14)	1 teaspoonful Potassium Baking Powder (page 14)
Juice of ½ lemon	Juice of ½ lemon
5 fl oz (140ml) yogurt or 1 beaten egg and milk to mix (3 fl oz)	⅔ cupful yogurt or 1 beaten egg and milk to mix (⅓ cupful)

1. Simmer the fruit with the spices and malt extract for approximately 10 minutes (making sure to keep the fruit well covered with water to stop it boiling dry) and leave to cool in the liquid.

2. Strain the cooled fruit and reserve the liquid. Heat the oven to 325°F/170°C (Gas Mark 3).

3. Rub the oil, flour and baking powder together. Add the fruit and lemon juice.

4. Mix with the yogurt or egg and add enough water from stewing the fruit to make a dropping consistency. It is important to look at the texture of the cake mixture, the stiffer it is the drier the cake will be, so make sure the mixture is soft and drops from the spoon readily.

5. Oil a 6-inch (15cm) square cake tin and put in the mixture. Bake in the pre-heated oven for 50 minutes. Leave to cool in the tin and cut when cooled.

GLAZED APPLE CAKE

Imperial (Metric)	American
1 lb (400g) eating apples	1 pound eating apples
1 tablespoonful cinnamon	1 tablespoonful cinnamon
4 oz (100g) dates	1 cupful dates
½ lb (200g) Sweet Pastry (page 110)	2 cupsful Sweet Pastry (page 110)
1 teaspoonful oil	1 teaspoonful oil
2 oz (50g) raisins	⅓ cupful raisins
Juice of 1 orange	Juice of 1 orange
Sugar-free apricot jam to glaze	Sugar-free apricot jam to glaze

1. Slice the apples but do not peel them.

2. Stew the dates in water until smooth and you can spread them.

3. Oil a 7-inch (18cm) sponge tin. Roll out half the pastry and place in the oiled tin.

4. Spread the pastry with the date purée.

5. Roll out the other half of the pastry and place over the date purée.

6. Spread the raisins and cinnamon over the pastry base.

7. Arrange the apples overlapping on the top.

8. Squeeze the orange juice on top of the apples and bake at 375°F/190°C (Gas Mark 5) for 35 minutes.

9. Glaze with the sugar-free apricot jam (heat the jam for easier glazing) and serve hot or cold.

VANILLA BITES

Imperial (Metric)	American
6 oz (150g) wholemeal flour	1½ cupsful wholewheat flour
4 tablespoonsful cold-pressed corn oil *or* ghee	4 tablespoonsful cold-pressed corn oil *or* ghee
4 tablespoonsful runny honey	4 tablespoonsful runny honey
1 tablespoonful vanilla essence	1 tablespoonful vanilla essence
2 oz (50g) soya flour	½ cupful soy flour
3 tablespoonsful water	3 tablespoonsful water

1. Grease a baking sheet. Heat the oven to 300°F/150°C (Gas Mark 2).

2. Mix all of the ingredients together.

3. Place in a piping bag and pipe the biscuits onto the baking tray. These biscuits spread, so space them well.

4. Bake in the preheated oven for approximately 12-15 minutes, until golden brown.

Note: The biscuits will still appear soft at the end of the cooking time and will become soggy if removed from the tray. Leave them to cool before removing from the tin. When cooled, biscuits baked with ghee will be crisper than those made with oil.

If you oil the spoon before measuring the honey, the honey will run off the spoon very easily.

GINGER BISCUITS

Imperial (Metric)	American
4 oz (100g) wholemeal flour	1 cupful wholewheat flour
1 teaspoonful Potassium Baking Powder (page 14)	1 teaspoonful Potassium Baking Powder (page 14)
1 teaspoonful cream of tartar	1 teaspoonful cream of tartar
1 teaspoonful ground ginger	1 teaspoonful ground ginger
2 oz (50g) ghee	¼ cupful ghee
1 tablespoonful honey	1 tablespoonful honey
1 tablespoonful malt	1 tablespoonful malt
1 teaspoonful molasses	1 teaspoonful molasses

1. Heat the oven to 375°F/190°C (Gas Mark 5). Oil two flat baking sheets.

2. Mix together the flour, baking powder, cream of tartar and ginger. Rub the ghee into the flour mixture.

3. Add the honey, malt and molasses (remember it is easier to measure 'sticky' foods if you oil the spoon first). This should give a soft dough.

4. Divide the mixture into fourteen equal pieces and roll into balls.

5. Place the ginger balls on the baking trays and press to flatten. The mixture spreads so space them well.

6. Cook in the pre-heated oven for 15 minutes — they should be a golden colour. Cool on the baking sheets.

SESAME COOKIES

Imperial (Metric)	American
¾ lb (300g) wholemeal flour	3 cupsful wholewheat flour
4 oz (100g) sesame seeds	¾ cupful sesame seeds
¼ teaspoonful Potassium Baking Powder (page 14)	¼ teaspoonful Potassium Baking Powder (page 14)
½ teaspoonful ginger	½ teaspoonful ginger
2½ fl oz (75ml) cold-pressed corn oil	5 tablespoonsful cold-pressed corn oil
2½ fl oz (75ml) maple syrup	5 tablespoonsful maple syrup

1. Seive half the flour and save the bran (keep it for cereal or for topping home-baked bread). Roast the sesame seeds.

2. Mix the two lots of flour, sesame seeds, baking powder and ginger together.

3. Mix the cold-pressed corn oil and maple syrup together.

4. Gently, with a fork mix the flour and oil ingredients together.

5. Add as little water as possible to make the pastry bind together — as in pastry making. Do not knead the mixture as this makes the cookies really tough. Roll out between two pieces of greaseproof paper. Cut into cookies.

6. Bake for 30 minutes at 350°F/180°C (Gas Mark 4) until light brown — they may feel a little soft but will firm on cooling.

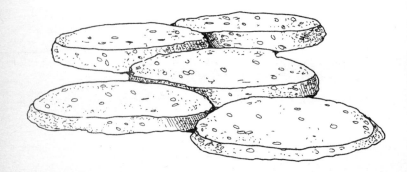

SCONE CAKE

Imperial (Metric)
4 oz (100g) mixed dried fruit
  (peaches, apples, pears, figs,
  dates)
½ pint (250ml) apple *or* grape juice
½ lb (200g) wholemeal flour
2 tablespoonsful cold-pressed
  sunflower oil
2 teaspoonsful Potassium Baking
  Powder (page 14) *or* 1 oz (25g)
  fresh yeast mixed with 2
  tablespoonsful water
1 oz (25g) creamed coconut
5 oz (125g) silken tofu *or* yogurt

American
1 cupful mixed dried fruit (peaches,
  apples, pears, figs, dates)
1⅓ cupsful apple *or* grape juice
2 cupsful wholewheat flour
2 tablespoonsful cold-pressed
  sunflower oil
2 teaspoonsful Potassium Baking
  Powder (page 14) *or* 2½
  tablespoonsful fresh yeast mixed
  with 2 tablespoonsful water
2½ tablespoonsful creamed coconut
⅔ cupful silken tofu *or* yogurt

1. Soak the fruit overnight in the apple or grape juice, strain but do not throw away the juice.

2. Heat the oven to 425°F/220°C (Gas Mark 7).

3. Rub together the flour, oil and raising agent until the mixture resembles breadcrumbs. Add the creamed coconut and rub in well.

4. Cut up the dried fruit and add to the flour mixture.

5. Mix together to form a soft dough with the tofu or yogurt — at this stage you may need to add a little of the reserved juice. If using tofu it should be liquidized.

6. Oil an 8-inch cake tin. Place the mixture in the tin and spread with a fork. If you have used yeast as your raising agent, leave the mixture to rise for 20 minutes. If you used baking powder, bake at once.

7. Bake for 20 minutes until golden-brown and leave to cool in the tin.

YOGURT SCONES
Makes 8

Imperial (Metric)	American
3 oz (75g) dried apricots	½ cupful dried apricots
½ pint (250ml) cold tea	1⅓ cupsful cold tea
1 tablespoonful cold-pressed corn oil	1 tablespoonful cold-pressed corn oil
½ lb (200g) wholemeal flour	2 cupsful wholewheat flour
2 teaspoonsful Potassium Baking Powder (page 14)	2 teaspoonsful Potassium Baking Powder (page 14)
¼ pint (140ml) yogurt	⅔ cupful yogurt
Sugar-free apricot jam to glaze (optional)	Sugar-free apricot jam to glaze (optional)

1. Soak the apricots in cold tea overnight and drain well.

2. Heat the oven to 425°F/220°C (Gas Mark 7).

3. Rub the oil into the flour and baking powder until it resembles breadcrumbs.

4. Chop the soaked apricots. Add them to the flour mixture and bind with the yogurt to form a soft dough.

5. Press the mixture out to 1-inch (2.5cm) thickness and cut with a 2-inch (5cm) cutter. Glaze the scones with sugar-free apricot jam if wished. Heat the jam, it spreads easier.

6. Oil a baking sheet and place the scones on it. Cook in the pre-heated oven for 15 minutes when the scones should have risen and be a golden-brown colour. Serve with puréed apricots and tahini (sesame seed butter).

5.

BREAD AND PASTRY

BASIC NO-SALT BREAD DOUGH
Makes 2×2 pound (1 kilo) loaves, plus 4 rolls or 1 pizza base

Imperial (Metric)	American
3 lbs (1.2 kilos) wholemeal flour	12 cupsful wholewheat flour
2 tablespoonsful cold-pressed sunflower oil	2 tablespoonsful cold-pressed sunflower oil
1½ pints (750ml) water	3¾ cupsful water
2 pieces kombu (sea vegetable)	2 pieces kombu (sea vegetable)
1 teaspoonful sweetener (this could be grape juice, grated carrot or apple juice)	1 teaspoonful sweetener (this could be grape juice, grated carrot or apple juice)
2 oz (50g) fresh *or* 1 oz (25g) dried yeast	¼ cupful fresh *or* 2 tablespoonsful dried yeast
1 teaspoonful kelp powder	1 teaspoonful kelp powder

1. In a bowl place half the flour and all the oil. Mix together well.

2. In a second bowl, place the water, kombu, sweetener and yeast and leave for 30 minutes.

3. Remove the kombu and mix the flour and liquid together to form a thick batter. Cover with cling film. Leave to double in size.

4. When risen, beat back and add 1 teaspoonful kelp powder, mix well.

5. Heat the oven to 425°F/220°C (Gas Mark 7).

Continued overleaf

6.   Add the rest of the flour at this stage and — this is very important
     — put down your spoon and knead the dough by hand. The drier
     the dough the harder and heavier the bread will be. You should
     have a soft dough.

7.   Shape the dough, place in two oiled loaf tins and leave to rise.
     The leftover dough can be shaped into rolls or used as a pizza base.

8.   Bake in the pre-heated oven for 40 minutes. When cooked the
     bread should sound hollow when tapped. Cool on a rack.

SAGE AND ONION BREAD

Imperial (Metric)	American
½ lb (200g) onions	8 ounces onions
1 oz (25g) fresh mint	1 ounce fresh mint
2 oz (50g) fresh sage	2 ounces fresh sage
2 lbs (800g) wholemeal flour	8 cupsful wholewheat flour
2 oz (50g) fresh or 1 oz (25g) dried yeast	¼ cupful fresh or 2 tablespoonsful dried yeast
3 tablespoonsful sesame seed oil (optional)	3 tablespoonsful sesame seed oil (optional)
Water to mix	Water to mix
2 oz (50g) oatmeal for the topping	½ cupful oatmeal for the topping

1. Chop the onion, mint and sage very finely and leave to stand overnight in a covered bowl.

2. Heat the oven to 350°F/180°C (Gas Mark 4).

3. Mix all the ingredients with enough water to form a cake-like mixture. It should drop from the spoon but not be too runny.

4. Oil a deep 10 × 8-inch (25 × 20cm) baking dish or tin. Place the mixture in the tin and spread with a fork.

5. Sprinkle the oatmeal on top and bake in the pre-heated oven for 35 minutes. Leave to cool in the tin. Cut into cubes and serve with soups or dips.

PINE AND CUMIN BREAD

Imperial (Metric)	American
2 oz (50g) pine kernels	1/3 cupful pine kernels
1 oz (25g) arame (sea vegetable)	1 ounce arame (sea vegetable)
1 pint (500ml) water	2 2/3 cupsful water
2 oz (50g) fresh or 1 oz (25g) dried yeast	1/4 cupful fresh or 2 tablespoonsful dried yeast
2 lbs (800g) wholemeal flour	8 cupsful wholewheat flour
2 oz (50g) cumin seeds	1/3 cupful cumin seeds

1. Oil two 2 lb (1 kilo) loaf tins. Heat oven to 400°F/200°C (Gas Mark 6).

2. Chop the pine kernels.

3. Soak the arame in the water.

4. Mix the flour, cumin and pine kernels together.

5. When the arame has become soft, strain it — the water only is used in this recipe, the arame can be used in salad or condiments.

6. Mix the yeast and sea vegetable water together and leave to stand until bubbles appear on the surface.

7. When it has bubbled, mix with the flour and other ingredients. You should have a mixture that resembles a rich fruit cake and be able to turn it over with a spoon.

8. Divide the mixture into 2×2 lb (1 kilo) loaf tins, leave to rise to the tops of the tins. Bake for 40 minutes in the pre-heated oven. The loaves will sound hollow when cooked, if tapped on the base. Leave to cool on a rack.

SOURDOUGH STARTER

Sourdough can be used in breadmaking to replace the yeast and at the same time produce a completely different flavour. There is no reason why sourdough bread should be heavy and thick in texture.

Imperial (Metric)	American
½ lb (200g) wholemeal flour	2 cupsful wholewheat flour
1 oz (25g) yeast	1 oz (25g) yeast
1 teaspoonful malt	1 teaspoonful malt
½ pint (250ml) water	1⅓ cupsful water

1. Day 1: Mix all the ingredients together and leave to stand.

2. Day 2: Mix in a further 4 ounces (100g) wholemeal flour.

3. Day 3: Add enough vegetable water to make the dough into a thick batter mixture.

4. Leave to stand for 8 days. The mixture is now ready for use as instructed in recipes.

5. There is no need to make new sourdough starter each time you want to make bread, you can take 6 ounces (150g) of dough out of the first and consecutive batches and put in more vegetable/sea vegetable water. The more the starter is used, the nicer the bread in flavour.

OLD ENGLISH SOURDOUGH

Imperial (Metric)	American
1 oz (25g) fresh thyme	1 ounce fresh thyme
1 oz (25g) fresh sage	1 ounce fresh sage
1 oz (25g) fresh chives	1 ounce fresh chives
1 clove garlic	1 clove garlic
¾ pint (425ml) sourdough starter*	2 cupsful sourdough starter*
1½ lbs (600g) wholemeal flour	6 cupsful wholewheat flour
2 tablespoonsful cold-pressed sesame oil	2 tablespoonsful cold-pressed sesame oil

1. Wash and chop the herbs and garlic into the sourdough starter the day before use.

2. In a bowl place half the flour and all the oil.

3. Add the sourdough starter, cover and leave to stand.

4. When the mixture has risen, add the rest of the flour, kneading the mixture to a smooth dough. Keep back 6 ounces (150g) dough.

5. Oil two 1 lb (500g) loaf tins.

6. Place dough in the tins and leave to stand until it has risen to the top of the tin.

7. Heat the oven to 375°F/190°C (Gas Mark 5).

8. Cook the sourdough bread in the pre-heated oven for 45 minutes.

9. To test it is cooked, tap the bottom of the loaf and it should sound hollow.

10. Place the reserved dough in vegetable water or sea vegetable water for the next time.

*To make ¾ pint (425ml/2 cupsful) starter, place the 6 ounces (150g) dough in a measuring jug, add liquid to the desired level and mash the dough and liquid together thoroughly.

SESAME RYE SOURDOUGH

Imperial (Metric)	American
1 oz (25g) jumbo oats	¼ cupful jumbo oats
½ lb (200g) sesame seeds	1½ cupsful sesame seeds
½ lb (200g) rye flour	2 cupsful rye flour
1 lb (400g) wholemeal flour	4 cupsful wholewheat flour
4 tablespoonsful cold-pressed sesame oil	4 tablespoonsful cold-pressed sesame oil
Sourdough starter, made up with vegetable water to measure 1 pint (500ml)	Sourdough starter, made up with vegetable water to measure 2⅔ cupsful

1. Roast the jumbo oats and sesame seeds and grind them so they are split, but not powdered.

2. Mix the flours, sesame seeds, oats, oil and sourdough starter together to form a soft dough. Take off 6 ounces (150g) of the dough to mix with vegetable or sea vegetable water for next time.

3. Oil a 9-inch (23cm) round cake tin.

4. Place the dough in the tin and leave to rise overnight in a cool, but not cold, place.

5. Heat the oven to 350°F/180°C (Gas Mark 5) and bake the bread for 45 minutes. Check it is cooked by tapping the bottom of the bread which should sound hollow.

6. Leave to cool in the tin. This is good served with garlic butter.

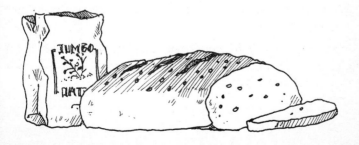

SALT-FREE PASTRY

Imperial (Metric)	American
½ lb (200g) wholemeal flour	2 cupsful wholewheat flour
6 tablespoonsful cold-pressed oil	6 tablespoonsful cold-pressed oil
Water to mix	Water to mix

1. Put the flour in a bowl and add the oil slowly, rubbing it into the flour. The mixture should resemble breadcrumbs.

2. In the bowl, divide the mixture in half and add water to one half of the 'breadcrumbs'. Add the water one tablespoonful at a time and gently mix the pastry together. Once one half of the mixture has come together, add no more water but press the remaining 'breadcrumbs' to the mixture. You should require only about 2 or 3 tablespoonsful water, so take care, it is this which can give you soft, crumbly pastry or dry, hard pastry.

3. Roll the pastry out between two pieces of greaseproof paper.

4. Place the pastry in the dish to be used by rolling up the pastry in one piece of the paper, turning it over into the dish and unrolling. If you are using the pastry for pasties or tarts, just cut out the shape required.

5. Once the dish is lined, leave the pastry to stand for 20 minutes (this stops the pastry shrinking and helps break down the phytic acid in wheat). Pre-heat the oven to 350°F/180°C (Gas Mark 4).

6. Bake the pastry for approximately 20 minutes. When cooking quiche, continue cooking until the filling is set.

7. When the pastry is cooked leave in the cooking container, but cool on a rack. This prevents the pastry going soggy.

Note: When choosing the oil to be used, give a little thought to the foods you are going to put with it.
- Sweet foods: cold-pressed corn oil.
- Mild foods (mushrooms, green peppers, potatoes, lentils, eggs, tofu): cold-pressed safflower or sunflower seed oil.
- Strong foods (onions, tomatoes, fennel): cold-pressed sesame seed oil.

For savoury pastry, 1 ounce (25g) of dried herbs can be added to the pastry mixture. Instead of using all oil in pastry making, ground nuts can be substituted. For 1 tablespoonful oil substitute 1 ounce (25g) ground nuts, but keep the proportion ⅔ oil to ⅓ nuts, or the pastry will be too dry.

If you know your flour to be very fresh you may find you need a little less oil.

SWEET PASTRY

Imperial (Metric)	American
1/3 pint (200ml) apple juice	3/4 cupful apple juice
3 fl oz (90ml) corn oil	1/3 cupful corn oil
1/2 lb (200g) wholemeal flour	2 cupsful wholewheat flour

1. Boil the apple juice and oil together.

2. When boiled, whisk the flour in. You need to be quick and vigorous if using a hand whisk.

3. Leave to cool.

4. When cooled, knead the mixture for approximately 2 minutes.

5. Chill for 1/2 hour and roll out between greaseproof paper, ready for use.

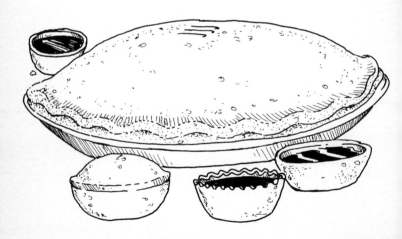

HERB PASTRY

Imperial (Metric)	**American**
2 tablespoonsful freshly chopped herbs	2 tablespoonsful freshly chopped herbs
2 tablespoonsful finely grated carrot	2 tablespoonsful finely grated carrot
½ lb (200g) wholemeal flour	2 cupsful wholewheat flour
4 tablespoonsful cold-pressed sesame oil	4 tablespoonsful cold-pressed sesame oil
Water to mix	Water to mix

1. Rub together the flour, oil and fresh herbs. Mix in the grated carrot.

2. Add the water as explained in notes on pastry making (page 108).

3. Press the mixture together. Do not knead. Roll out between two pieces of greaseproof paper. Use for savoury dishes.

6.

CHEESEMAKING

Utensils
Make sure all utensils used in cheesemaking are very clean, otherwise the cheese can taste bitter. Stainless steel and plastic are best for cheesemaking, avoid the use of wood, aluminium and enamelled cooking utensils.

Cloths
The tradition of using muslin or dripping bags was brought about as they are the types of cloth that can be boiled. It is now easy to obtain fine plastic mesh sieves and strainers for dripping. They are much easier to clean than cloths.

Moulds
I find it easiest to use small plastic moulds, so two or three different types of cheese can be presented at one time. When making large quantities of cheese in large moulds they are not as pretty when presented on the cheese board, but keep the cheese much better.

HOME-MADE COTTAGE CHEESE
Makes approximately 10 oz (250g/1¼ cupsful)

Imperial (Metric)
2 pints (500ml) milk — goat's or cow's
Juice of 1 lemon

American
5 cupsful milk — goat's or cow's
Juice of 1 lemon

1. Heat the milk gently in a stainless steel pan.

2. Add the lemon juice and leave to stand until cooled.

3. When cooled, strain through a muslin cloth or fine nylon sieve, cover well and leave to drip overnight.

4. Turn the cheese into plastic trays (of the type used to stack yogurt and cheese cartons in supermarkets), the bottom of which have been pricked with a needle to allow for further drainage.

5. You can make the cheese firmer by placing weights on top and pressing. (It is at this stage that salt is added to cheese.) Instead of adding salt, try one of the following flavourings.

RED PEPPER AND CHILLI CHEESE

Imperial (Metric)
1 small red pepper
½ large chilli (the larger the chilli
   the milder it is)
1 quantity Home-Made Cottage
   Cheese (page 113)

American
1 small red pepper
½ large chili (the larger the chili the
   milder it is)
1 quantity Home-made Cottage
   Cheese (page 113)

1. Chop half of the pepper and all of the chilli into small pieces and slice the rest of the pepper into circles. Mix the small pieces of pepper and chilli together with the cheese.

2. Arrange the pepper rings in the bottom of the plastic trays.

3. Cover with the cheese and press down until you can get no more in.

4. Place a piece of waxed paper on top and keep in a refrigerator, freezer, or leave to dry out further in a warm, dry place (if you use your airing cupboard your clothes will start to smell of cheese!).

PINEAPPLE CHEESE

Imperial (Metric)
½ small fresh pineapple
1 quantity Home-made Cottage
   Cheese (page 113)

American
½ small fresh pineapple
1 quantity Home-made Cottage
   Cheese (page 113)

1. Slice the top quarter of the pineapple into rings and cut out the fibrous centre. Cut off the woody skin. Cut the pineapple rings into pieces.

2. Arrange the pineapple pieces decoratively in the bottom of the moulds and round the edges.

3. Chop the rest of the pineapple into very small pieces and add to the cheese.

4. Cover the pineapple with the cheese, place waxed paper over the top and press. Stand the moulds in a tray to catch the liquid.

5. Keep pressing the cheese for 24 hours — this is important as so much liquid comes out of the pineapple and can make the cheese sloppy.

6. Serve with rye crackers or fresh fruit.

GARLIC AND CELERY LACTIC CHEESE

Imperial (Metric)	**American**
2 pints (1 litre) yogurt	5 cupsful yogurt
3 cloves garlic	3 cloves garlic
3 sticks celery	3 stalks celery
3 oz (75g) sesame seeds	⅔ cupful sesame seeds

1. Place the yogurt in a muslin or dripping bag and allow to drip for 48 hours.

2. Peel and chop the garlic very finely.

3. Wash and chop the celery very finely.

4. Mix the celery and garlic into the dripped yogurt, place in a clean dripping cloth or bag and leave to drip for a further 48 hours.

5. Place in plastic moulds (see Cottage Cheese recipe, page 113).

6. Grind the sesame seeds.

7. Cover the small pats of cheese with ground sesame seeds.

8. Freeze or keep the cheese in a refrigerator.

HERB CHEESE

Imperial (Metric)	American
4 oz (100g) fresh mixed herbs (sage, borage, sweet savory thyme, mint, anise)	4 ounces fresh mixed herbs (sage, borage, sweet savory, thyme mint, anise)
2 pints (1 litre) yogurt	5 cupsful yogurt

1. Place the yogurt in a muslin or dripping bag.

2. Wash and chop the herbs very finely.

3. Dab the herbs with kitchen paper to dry off the water.

4. Add the herbs to the cheese and put back into a clean muslin or dripping bag.

5. Leave to drip for 48 hours.

6. Spoon into plastic moulds (see Cottage Cheese recipe, page 113).

7. Press the cheese into the moulds and cover with waxed paper.

8. Freeze or keep the cheese in a refrigerator.

CHEESE FLAVOURINGS

Cottage Cheese, per 10 ounces (250g), add:
3 ounces (55g) finely chopped onion *and* 1 tablespoonful chopped sage.
2 ounces (50g) candied peel.
3 ounces (75g) chives *and* ½ ounce (12g) rosemary, chopped finely.
4 ounces (100g) spring onions (scallions), chopped very finely.
1 ounce (25g) ground black pepper.
3 ounces (75g) fresh fennel, chopped finely, *with* 1 teaspoonful fennel seeds.
1 ounce (12g) carraway seeds.
4 ounces (100g) freshly chopped fennel *and* 1 tablespoonful honey.

Lactic Cheese, per 10 ounces (250g), add:
1 ounce (25g) cumin seeds *and* 2 ounces (50g) sesame seeds.
1 ounce (25g) cumin and coriander seeds, mixed.
1 ounce (25g) limdo (curry) leaves.
1 teaspoonful celery seeds.
1-inch (2.5cm) fresh horseradish, grated very finely.
½-inch (1cm) fresh ginger *and* 1 large grated apple.
Line plastic moulds with bay leaves *or* lemon balm.

GLOSSARY

Arame: A seaweed reconstituted by placing in water. It is very rich in minerals.

Asafoetida: Another name for asafoetida is *hing* or *devil's dung*. It has the most distinguished smell and should be used in moderation in cooking. It is made from the dried gummy juice of a large perennial plant grown in Asia, Turkey and Afghanistan. It is a member of the *ferula* family.

Buckwheat spaghetti — also called Soba.

Bulgar: Cracked roasted wheat.

Cold-pressed oil: This refers to the type of manufacture of the oil from the original seed. It is superior in nutrative value to refined oil.

Cold-pressed corn oil: used in baking.

Cold-pressed sunflower oil }
Cold-pressed Safflower oil } Two general purpose oils

Cold-pressed sesame oil: for sautéeing vegetables and salad dressings.

Virgin olive oil: salad dressings.

Corn: also called maize.

Eggs: You can substitute eggs with 2 tablespoonsful of soya flour mixed to a paste with water.

Fenugreek: A seed with a spicy almost curry flavour. Sometimes called *methi*. It can be bought as a fresh leaf, seed or powder.

Garam Masala: A mixture of cinnamon, cumin, coriander, allspice, nutmeg and caraway powder.

Ghee: Clarified butter (page 24).

Ginger: Used as a fresh root or in powder form.

Gomasio: Sesame seed salt.

Gram: The name given to bean flours made from chick peas or moong beans.

Green Lentils: Whole lentils sometimes called continental lentils.

Haricot Beans: A small white bean, better known as baked beans.

Juniper Berries: A small berry better known for their use in gin making.

Kelp: A ground sea vegetable obtainable in powder form.

Kombu: Sea vegetable.

Kudzu: An arrowroot-type flour obtained from a plant tuber.

Malt: A thick sticky sweetener made from sprouted barley.

Masala Dal: A collection of spices — milder than curry powder.

Mekabu: Sea vegetable — this is the frond of wakame.

Millet: A grain obtainable in flake or whole form.

Miso: A paste made from fermented soya beans.

Mustard Seed: Available in yellow or black seeds, ground or whole seeds.

Okra: Also known as 'ladies fingers' — a green pod vegetable that can be used as a thickening agent.

Pine Nuts: The kernels from pine nuts — a small white tasty nut.

Rice Vinegar: A light vinegar made from rice.

Sourdough: A raising agent made from sour grain or flour.

Tahini: Is a butter made from sesame seeds. Light tahini is easier to use in cooking. Dark tahini is made from roasted sesame seeds and takes on the colour and texture of mud, but has a wonderful flavour.

Tamarind: It is also known as the Indian Date, it is the fleshy part of the pod from a leguminous tree that grows in East Africa and the West Indies. The pod is approx. 6-8 inches (15-20cm) long, containing seeds and the tamarind pulp, which is a black sticky mess. It also has mild laxative properties.

Tamarino Flowers: A thick, slightly bitter tasting, sticky interior of the tamarind peel.

Tharka: When spices are added to Ghee.

Tofu: Is a curd made from soya beans. It is made from the 'milk' of the soya bean and does not include any of the fibre, therefore it is low in calories and the complex starches which can sometimes be responsible for causing flatulence. Silken tofu is easily available in vacuumed cartons.

Turmeric: Is a rhizome belonging to the ginger family. It is peeled, washed and diced before being ground to a fine powder. It contains approximately 30-40 per cent starch and is best known for giving colour to curries and rice dishes.

Yeast: When substituting dried yeast for fresh yeast halve the quantities in the recipe.

APPENDIX

THE SODIUM CONTENT OF FOODS

The Sodium Content of Dried Beans and Tofu

	100g portions
Broad (Windsor) beans: boiled	20 mg
Butter (Lima) beans: raw	62 mg
boiled	16 mg
Haricot (navy) beans: raw	43 mg
boiled	15 mg
baked	480 mg
Mung beans: raw *or* as green gram	28 mg
Red kidney beans: raw	40 mg
cooked	6 mg
Lentils: raw	36 mg
split and boiled	12 mg
Peas: dried	38 mg
boiled	13 mg
split	38 mg
boiled	14 mg
Chick peas (garbanzo beans):	
as gram flour *or* raw	40 mg
cooked	6 mg
Borlotti (pinto) beans: raw	19 mg
cooked	10 mg
Soya beans: cooked	3 mg
Tofu	6 mg

The Sodium Content of Sauces, Pickles and Flavourings

See pages 12-13.
Miso: see page 17.

The Sodium Content of Dairy Products

Milk: see page 11.
Butter: see page 14.
Cheese: see page 15.

The Sodium Content of Vegetables

per 100g

Beans: French (snap), boiled	3 mg
Runner (green), raw	2 mg
boiled	1 mg
Beansprouts	5 mg
Beetroot: raw	84 mg
boiled	64 mg
Broccoli: raw	12 mg
cooked	6 mg
Brussels sprouts: raw	4 mg
boiled	2 mg
Cabbage: red, raw	32 mg
Savoy, raw	23 mg
boiled	8 mg
White, raw	7 mg
Winter, raw	7 mg
boiled	4 mg
Carrots: old, raw	95 mg
boiled	50 mg
young, boiled	23 mg
canned	280 mg
Cauliflower: raw	8 mg
boiled	4 mg
Celeriac: boiled	28 mg

Celery: raw	140 mg
boiled	67 mg
Chicory (Endive in U.S.A.): raw	7 mg
Cucumber: raw	13 mg
Endive (Chicory in U.S.A.): raw	10 mg
Horseradish: raw	8 mg
Leeks: raw	9 mg
boiled	6 mg
Lettuce: raw	9 mg
Marrow (summer squash): raw	1 mg
boiled	1 mg
Mushrooms: raw	2 mg
Mustard and Cress	19 mg
Okra	7 mg
Onions: raw	10 mg
boiled	7 mg
spring (scallions)	13 mg
Parsley	33 mg
Parsnips: raw	17 mg
cooked	4 mg
Peas: fresh	1 mg
boiled	Trace
canned	230 mg
processed	330 mg
Peppers, green: raw	2 mg
boiled	2 mg
Potatoes: old, raw	7 mg
boiled	3 mg
baked	8 mg
chips	12 mg
new, boiled	41 mg
Pumpkin	1 mg
Radishes	59 mg
Salsify	8 mg
Seakale	4 mg
Spinach	120 mg
Spring greens (collards): boiled	10 mg

Swedes (rutabaga): raw	52 mg
cooked	14 mg
Sweetcorn: raw	1 mg
cooked	1 mg
canned	310 mg
Sweet potatoes: raw	19 mg
cooked	18 mg
Tomatoes: raw	3 mg
canned	29 mg
Turnips: raw	58 mg
boiled	28 mg
Turnip tops: boiled	7 mg
Watercress: raw	60 mg

The Sodium Content of Nuts and Seeds

In 100g portions (without shells)

Almonds	6 mg
Brazils	2 mg
Chestnuts	11 mg
Hazelnuts	1 mg
Coconut	17 mg
Peanuts	6 mg
Walnuts	3 mg
Sesame seeds	67 mg
Pumpkin seeds	—
Sunflower seeds	37 mg

INDEX